An
ACCIDENTAL PIONEER

A Farm Girl's Drive to the Finish …

An
ACCIDENTAL PIONEER

A Farm Girl's Drive to the Finish ...

Lorene McCormick Burkhart

Hawthorne Publishing

ISBN 0-9787167-0-1

Published in the United States by Hawthorne Publishing. For information and
ordering, contact the publisher at
15601 Oak Road
Carmel, Indiana 46033
317-867-5183

For more information about the author, see the website www.LoreneBurkhart.com,
or she may be contacted at Lorene@LoreneBurkhart.com

Printed in the United States

Dust jacket design by Paul Wilson Design, Inc.
Interior design by Cindy Kelley of cindykelley@mac.com

DEDICATION

*To my parents, Emma and Clarence McCormick,
the original "Accidental Pioneers."*

ACKNOWLEDGMENTS

Memories are selective. This story is of course told from my own viewpoint, but it's not exclusively my story, so I enlisted the aid of several relatives in order to glean the most accurate information.

I would like to thank my brothers Jim, Don, and Ed McCormick, with whom I shared many a chuckle as one of us would exclaim, "No, it didn't happen that way!" Equally generous with their recollections were my cousins Alice Ann Osborne Ready, Imo Jeanne Osborne Williams, Gladys Neal Rumer, Evelyn Bobe Cofer, and John Henry Bobe.

CONTENTS

I was born and grew up in southern Indiana, on a farm situated at the highest point of an area bordered by two rivers, the Wabash on the west and the White on the east.

We never used these rivers for recreation, and rarely even for fishing; they were merely boundaries. For us, the White River held no fascination, other than whether or not it would rise above its banks and flood whatever crops we had planted in the bottom land. Illinois was just across the Vincennes bridge that spanned the Wabash, but I seldom traveled there. We had just about everything we needed right where we were.

On the surface, growing up on that farm between the two rivers was serene and simple. As is often the case, however, things may not be as they appear, and just as a river has unseen currents running beneath its surface, below my family's surface were some rather complicated dynamics. Only through the perspectives of adulthood and my own experiences have I begun to perceive and understand those dynamics, and how they impacted everything I have done. I learned that with solid values, creativity, hard work, and strong faith in God, one can break beyond any limits. I learned that life is whatever you choose to make of it.

My careers have ranged from teaching home economics to working in public relations and marketing, to being one of the first female executives of a major American corporation. I also worked extensively in radio and television, beating Martha Stewart to the broadcast "how-to" genre in home and "economic" issues. Ultimately I reached a point where I was blessed to be able to work as a volunteer in my community with various organizations designed to enrich and improve the lives of others. The work may be for no pay, but I have been compensated by the tremendous satisfaction found in giving back.

My experiences have been unbelievable, nothing like I ever visualized as a girl growing up on a farm, a girl who wrote in high school that her career goal was to be a home economics extension agent!

All of my achievements were enriching, but what has always been most important to me was my family, the one I was born into and the one I eventually had of my own.

Along the way, during my seventy-plus years, numerous men and women — boyfriends, girlfriends, teachers, bosses, colleagues and coworkers — have had a tremendous effect on me.

And to think it all began on a farm. This is a story of a farm girl's life, drive, and perseverance. This is my story.

I wasn't named "Strutsie" when I was born. It was a nickname I picked up when I was about three years old because everyone in my family thought it fit me perfectly. It was derived from a character in the children's card game, "Old Maid," a little girl named Mandy Struts. The picture on the card showed her with blond hair and blue eyes, playing dress-up in grown-up high heels and a saucy hat perched atop her curls. As my mother explained it, they thought Mandy Struts looked a lot like me. A favorite snapshot of me at about age three backs that up: There I am, all decked out in my mother's hat and shoes, with the added panache of a girdle pulled up over my frock. Thus I became "Struts" or "Strutsie," and the nickname endures yet today by those who knew me then.

It's a widely held belief that we're born with a lot of our personality and that we only refine it as we age. I guess that's why the Struts name has stuck. (My fondness for playing dress-up has remained a lifelong passion, except now it's called "shopping and showing.")

How do we evolve into who we are? What are the forces that shape us into the kind of persons we become?

We hear endless debates about nature versus nurture and what makes people tick, but the answers seem always elusive. I believe that much of our character comes from where we grow up, the people, the history, and the culture of our childhood. Knox County, the place between the two rivers where I was raised, is one of the richest historical and cultural areas in the Midwest, the birthplace of many of the influences that shaped the region. I'm proud to be a product of that environment.

We can't thank our forebears for providing our rich heritage, but

I hope to express my gratitude in this book by presenting a look at my history. My childhood, my family, and how we lived provided my foundation, and I used the values and strengths of that foundation to create what I am today. I've discovered also that as we peek into the crackled mirror of life, we see not only reflections of our past, but also glimpses of our future.

In some respects my story is much like that of many women who grew up on farms in the days before and during World War II. Women then expected traditional worlds of home and children and the role of being wife and helpmate for the family's endeavors. My family was nontraditional, however, and my life has continued to be nontraditional in ways that have amazed me. But in spite of the forces that drive me along unexpected routes, at heart I am and will always be a farm girl.

I
FARM GIRL

Muncie

Vincennes

New Harmony

CHAPTER 1

Genes and Geography

The Creation of Character

When my father, Clarence James McCormick, died on January 30, 1983, news of his passing made the front page of the *Knox County Daily News*, along with a story of his life that occupied one-third of page seven. His obituary also appeared in *The Indianapolis Star* and *The Indianapolis News* and several other state and regional publications. His death was picked up by the UPI wire service and noted nationwide in such newspapers as *The New York Times*, *The Courier-Journal* (Louisville), and *The Tribune* (San Diego).

Dad was born into a farm family that lived near the town of Decker in southwestern Knox County, about fifteen miles south of Vincennes. So what was it about a "country boy" from southern Indiana that made his death national news?

It's understandable that his obituary would have been picked up by state and regional papers. My dad had been active in the Knox County community, working as a young adult in local farm programs, then moving up to state organizations such as the Agriculture Adjustment Administration (AAA) and the Purdue University extension program. In time, however, he moved to a position of national importance as chief of the Corn and Soybean Section of the Commodity Credit Corporation, a branch of the Department of Agriculture in Washington, D.C. Most significant, however, was that in 1950 he was appointed Under Secretary of Agriculture by President Harry S. Truman.

How does a man from a tiny rural Indiana community come to

be such an important national figure, a part of the president's staff? Anyone who knew my dad would never wonder at that. Reaching for high goals was part of his nature. It was something bred into him from childhood, something that was an intrinsic part of his family makeup. It was also something that he passed along to his children, for which I am profoundly grateful.

My brothers and I learned so much from our parents, and are living examples of the successful blending of nature *and* nurture. There surely is more to what a person becomes, what they make of themselves, that is beyond the combination of genes and environment. I believe that true success requires courage, creativity, and determination, as well as a willingness to work really hard for what you want. I was fortunate to learn these traits from my family, but ultimately, what I made of my life was up to me alone.

I joined the Clarence and Emma Bobe McCormick family during a record-breaking heat wave on Wednesday, July 11, 1934. Weather conditions notwithstanding, my parents were thrilled that, after having two sons, their new baby was a girl. Several names had been considered for their darling daughter, with Mother favoring Lois. Dad prevailed with Lorene. I'm happy for that; I have nothing against the name "Lois," but that wouldn't have been my first choice, either. The name Lorene may have come from my dad's cousin's wife or from a neighbor lady, Lorene Pea. My middle name, Joan, apparently was a mutual choice, and was pronounced with two syllables, "Jo-Ann." (All of my brothers were named for family members: James, Donald, and Edward.)

Anyone who's ever been to southern Indiana in the middle of the summer knows that it gets hot and humid — somewhere between steamy and really unbearable. According to Indiana weather statistics, a record high of one hundred and six degrees was recorded on July 21, 1934, ten days after my birth. There was no such thing as home air-conditioning back then, so Mother had to make do with hoping for a breeze from the open windows as her labor progressed.

Hospitals back then weren't air-conditioned, either, so going to one would have provided little if any relief. That likely wasn't even considered an option, as women were rarely hospitalized for something as mundane as childbirth in those days. My mother gave birth to all four of her children at home, each time attended by our great-uncle on my dad's side of the family, Dr. Hubert D. McCormick, known affectionately to us as "Uncle Doc." Whenever Mother went into labor, Dad would summon him and Uncle Doc would crank up his Model A or Model T and drive the seven miles from Vincennes to tend to her. All the necessary items for childbirth would have been assembled before the doctor's arrival: extra sheets or other bedding placed under the mother-to-be, swaddling clothes for the newborn infant, cloths to take the afterbirth, a nearby cradle, and a sharp knife for cutting the cord. There was very little in the way of helpful devices such as sophisticated painkillers and surgical equipment in the doctor's black bag, so I can only imagine that the expectant mother probably prayed for a short labor and uneventful delivery. My birth was evidently one of those uneventful ones, even though my mother, who was thirty-two at the time, had experienced difficulties during the pregnancy.

I was an average-sized baby — seven and a half pounds, twenty-one inches long — who happily took to my mother's breast and over the next few weeks and months became chubby and healthy. Like most babies, I had practically no hair, just a little peach fuzz, and I had big blue eyes like both my parents.

I once asked my older brother Jim what he remembered about the day of my birth, but he was short on any details. The story Mother always told, however, was that when he learned he had a baby sister, he let out a whoop and said, "Oh, good! I won't have to dry the dishes anymore." He must have been horribly disappointed, because he was almost ten years older than I, and by the time I took up the dish towel he was long gone. My other brother, Don, who was four when I was born, had no expectations for his little sister, nor did he seem to care one way or the other about my being there — an attitude that continued for several years, I might add.

Only eighteen months after I was born, my younger brother Eddie came along. My other brothers were too much older than I for us to ever be really close as youngsters, but Eddie and I were like peas in a pod, practically inseparable. Wherever I went, he went. He became my best buddy, my soul mate, and that close relationship never changed.

It was around 1929, when my oldest brother Jimmie was four years old, and five years before I was born, that my parents moved to the farm they eventually would buy, after renting it for a while, the farm where I was born and would call home for twenty-one years.

The farmhouse, a clapboard structure built around 1900, wasn't large by today's standards, and it certainly wasn't luxurious, but it served our family for more than fifty years. We didn't get electricity until around 1940, but before then the house at least had indoor plumbing to a pump for water, but didn't eliminate trips to an outhouse.

It was a simple one-story home with a porch extending across the front; the yard was enclosed by hedges and spirea bushes grew against the house, which gave the property a neat, settled look. Like many homes of that era, ours was built in shotgun style, with the main rooms lined up front to back: living room (or front room, as we called it), dining room, and kitchen. The bedrooms, and later, the bathroom, were along the sides of the main living area, accessed by doors scattered here and there. It seemed like the interior was nothing but doors, but without central hallways, there was no other way to get from one room to another. Those doors were seldom closed, which facilitated better air circulation, really welcome during the hot summer months.

Before we had central heating, we rarely occupied the front room, and the dining room, with its lovely bay window overlooking mother's flower garden, was used only when we had company. The heart of the home was the kitchen. It was there that we cooked, ate, and socialized. The center of the room was dominated by a large wooden table with an oilcloth tablecloth and six chairs. In the early days we used a large, wood-burning stove for cooking. Later, after electricity came in, the stove was replaced with an electric range, as well as a refrigerator. Linoleum covered the floor, and the walls were lined with built-in cabinets, a double sink with hot and cold running water, and a counter topped with a Formica-like surface wrapped around part of the room. A door between the refrigerator and stove led into a small pantry that was used to hold store-bought canned goods and odds and ends. In time, a washer was installed in that tiny area, and later, but not until I was in high school, a dryer. The kitchen also served as Mother's "office." I remember her sitting evenings at the kitchen table, writing checks for the bills that she kept organized by skewering them onto a hook in the wall near the back door.

The back door led to a roomy, enclosed back porch with large windows. This provided extra storage space and also served as a mud room where the men could clean their shoes, hang up their hats and jackets, and wash up at a sink there so they wouldn't track dirt through the house or get the bathroom grimy. Just about everyone came and went through that back entrance. When we kids weren't in school, we were in and out constantly, and when Dad was home, he just about wore out his voice calling, "Shut the door!"

The back porch also contained an enamel-top work table that was used to weigh and brush the eggs from our chickens before they were carefully placed into their fifteen-dozen-per-case containers for delivery to the hatchery on Saturdays. The table, and later, a countertop next to the sink, were catchalls — we seldom saw the tops of them. Mother kept a stool nearby so she could sit while she cut up chickens, prepared cucumbers for making pickles, washed fresh vegetables, and skinned rabbits after the men had been hunting. Any kind of messy food preparation job — and on the farm there were plenty! — was relegated to the back porch. Because it wasn't heated, though, it didn't get much winter usage, except for storage.

As was typical in farm houses, we had a cellar, and in its cool depths were shelves to hold jar after jar of home-canned fruits and vegetables, potatoes grown in the garden, a metal can of the lard we used for frying and baking, and bushel baskets full of fruit jars as they were emptied throughout the year. The empty jars always managed to accumulate a considerable quantity of dead bugs over the months, and during canning season it was my job to empty the little carcasses out and wash the jars.

The coal-fired furnace that kept us warm through the winter months occupied a second room in the cellar, along with the pile of coal that was unloaded through a chute in a nearby window. Mother always got up long before we did and shoveled coal into the furnace to heat the house for her children. I remember standing over the register in my bedroom on those cold mornings and watching my nightgown billow out as that delicious heat rose up around my legs.

<hr />

I was too young when Eddie came along to remember how I reacted to the little newcomer, but I doubt that I was very excited about his arrival. Before long, he was replacing me on my mother's lap, so I had to find another lap. Fortunately, Dorothy Meyer, the young woman Mother hired to help out with the house and the children, had a genuine affection for me. She let me rummage through her clothing for my "dress-up" clothes, and always made sure that my hair was fixed just so with a perky hair bow. Little Strutsie loved being the only girl, and I basked in the attention I got from my dad whenever I had a new frock and he would say, "Let's see you twirl around in your pretty dress." I wasn't very old before my older brothers started grudgingly calling me "The Princess." Royal status notwithstanding, Eddie was absolutely adorable with his tow head, big dimpled smile, and happy disposition, and he gave me some stiff competition. Mother called him her "Eddie Boy." He was, after all, her "baby," the last child.

I was never jealous of Eddie, though, and loved having my own little play partner who was more than willing to do my bidding. I wouldn't say that I was more mischievous than any other child, but even so, it turned out that little Eddie often was led astray by his big sister. We lived on the corner of a T in the road called South Hart Street Road. Cars would slow to a crawl as they reached the end of the road where they had to choose from three options: our driveway or the left or right road, as a fence and field loomed straight ahead. It was somewhere in that vicinity that my mother discovered Eddie, about age two at the time, with his bucket and shovel, picking up rocks in the middle of the gravel road, with me "supervising." It probably wasn't a good choice, although he did survive, but I do recall a stern warning never to let it happen again!

Not too many things are better than really good country cooking, and my mother was outstanding in that area. Her noodles, a farm-meal staple that she always served with stewed chicken, were wonderful. I remember watching her make them, piling the flour into a mound on the work surface, and mixing in eggs and water until the dough was just right. She'd then roll the dough out into a large, thin sheet and let it dry on waxed-paper-covered newspaper before cutting it into strips about one-eighth- to one-fourth inch wide. The noodles would be shaken out and the whole shebang would be placed on top of the upright piano in the front room, away from little hands. Or so Mother thought. About as soon as her back was turned, I'd climb to the top of the piano and toss the noodles down to my innocent sidekick Eddie.

My mother never used measuring cups or spoons when she made her famous noodles — or anything else, for that matter. Those old-fashioned cooks used a handful of this, a teacup full of that, and a pinch or dash of the other. I, on the other hand, and because of my home ec training, am a strict measuring cup and spoon kind of gal.

Mother's Noodles

⅔ to 1 cup flour, plus extra for flouring the board

1 egg, lightly beaten

Water to fill half an egg shell

Salted broth from one chicken

Sift the flour into a mound and make a well in the middle. Add the egg and the water to the well. Carefully work just a little flour at a time into the egg and water, just until the dough becomes a soft ball. Place the dough on a floured board and knead gently just until smooth. Add flour as needed, but be careful not to add so much that the dough gets too stiff and hard.

Roll dough out on a lightly floured surface into a large sheet about ⅛ inch thick, keeping just enough flour underneath that it doesn't stick. Spread out a newspaper and cover it with waxed paper. Sprinkle about two tablespoons of flour on the waxed paper and carefully transfer the noodle dough to it. (If necessary, the dough can be rolled a bit more to keep it flat and smooth.) Let the dough dry about 3 or 4 hours, then cut in narrow strips. (The noodles can be dried further, until thoroughly dry, and kept for weeks.)

Bring a pot of chicken broth to a brisk boil. Add the noodles, a few at a time. Let broth return to a boil, then reduce heat and cook 30 to 50 minutes, or until the noodles are done.

Life on our farm in the late 1930s was tranquil for us young children. During the winter months we spent our time mostly playing indoors, but once warm weather came, we were outdoors, coming inside long enough to eat and sleep. I had a small rubber doll, probably about eight inches tall, that was a constant companion. She accompanied Eddie and me on a series of hijinks, such as climbing the windmill just to jump down, and testing my balance by walking the six-inch ledge of the horse trough to see if I could keep from falling into the brackish water. We also enjoyed playing in the grain bin. We would climb up to a small ledge in a corner of the bin and jump into the grain. Needless to say, we would be covered with dust from head to toe by the time we were done playing. Next on our "rounds," we would go from the grain bin to the barn. There we would look for mice nests so we could play with the tiny babies before the cats found them.

To say that many of our activities were risky would be an understatement. We never stopped to consider that one of our leaps from the windmill or a tree could have resulted in broken bones, nor that we could have sunk into the corn in the grain bin and suffocated. Like most young children, we saw ourselves as invincible, and the assorted scrapes and bruises we got from our adventures were simply the price we paid for our fun.

Mother never discouraged us from our exploits. She never warned us to not do something because we might get hurt, nor did she ever admonish me to refrain from any activity because it might not be considered "ladylike." The unsaid message was that if we got into a scrape, we'd have to figure out ourselves how to get out of it. Because of this, I grew up never once thinking that perhaps I couldn't do certain things or attempt challenges because I might fail. I always saw myself as equal to "one of the boys" when it came to an adventure.

My adventuresome spirit and enthusiasm for risk-taking was curtailed only by occasional illness. Most notable was a very bad bout with scarlet fever at age two. Then I had my tonsils removed around the age of six, a procedure that was considered standard preventive medicine in those days, with everyone having their tonsils removed at a young age, whether or not they were a problem. We encountered the usual childhood diseases — chicken pox, measles, and whooping cough. Fortunately, we were spared smallpox, as there was an immunization for it.

We, like most farm children in that era, had very few toys. I don't recall crayons or coloring books until I started school. I do recall, in addition to my rubber doll, a "talking" doll with a large, round, plaster head with painted-on hair, and eyes that opened and closed. She had a stuffed cloth body and plaster arms and legs, and said "mama" when you tipped her backward. Because she was about twenty-two or twenty-four inches tall, I was able to dress her in newborn-size booties, dresses, and caps, castoffs from Eddie, no doubt. She was not as durable as the rubber doll, and she later suffered a severe gash in the back of her head. I had a little cedar chest to store her spare clothes and a small bed for her naps.

I also had a play kitchen stove and sink set. They were small, about a couple of feet or so high and didn't actually function. The play cooking equipment included a set of aluminum pans and a small cast-iron skillet, exactly like the big one Mother used daily. Little Eddie was my playtime assistant until he grew old enough to be interested in more boy-type activities than pretend cooking. He and I passed countless hours climbing the apple trees in the small orchard beyond the chicken yard and pretending our enclosures of branches were our "houses." We'd often stay there until Mother came looking for us when it was time to come in. Sometimes we would see rabbits in the orchard and Mother would tell us to put salt on their tails to catch them. It took us awhile to figure out the humor behind that advice.

A peddler who stopped by once every week provided a welcome break in our routine. Gaylord Meyer drove a small, enclosed truck that he kept stocked with food staples and a few treats for children, such as lollipops and penny candy. While Gaylord was inside the house talking to Mother, Eddie and I often would "visit" the truck. More than once, Mother had to pay for candy we had unwrapped for either a look or a lick. Fortunately, Gaylord thought it was amusing and didn't seem to be upset by our antics, understandable since it was a sure sale.

Farm youngsters almost never had bicycles, which didn't really matter because all the roads were gravel and not easy to ride on with bikes. We did have a few "pedal-and-push" toys, such as my little scooter, which could be used on our concrete sidewalks around the house, and a swing hung by two ropes attached to a low limb on one of the large maple trees in the side yard. We pretended to fish in the farm ponds with hand-fashioned fishing poles made from tree branches. Other times would find us playing kick-the-can, and we spent evenings until bedtime playing hide-and-seek in the dark after plastering ourselves with the lights from lightning bugs. We were very creative in our play.

I had no sisters, and fortunately for me, my brothers never excluded me from their games. I learned at an early age to hold my own in a man's world (good training for my later careers). We often played softball or baseball in the front yard, using the trees or bushes as bases and staying well away from the house in order to avoid hitting the ball into the windows. We knew that breaking a window definitely would not be a good idea. During one game, I stepped a little too close to the batter in my role as catcher and took a bat hit in the center of my forehead. Mother heard the crack from inside the house and came running when she heard me howling. Poor Don, the batter, proclaimed his innocence, saying that it was my fault for getting too close. Fortunately, all I suffered was a headache for a while and a lifetime dent in my forehead.

Sundays after church gave me a brief reprieve from boy games if one of my girl cousins came to visit or if Alice Ann Osborne, a cousin and my best girlfriend, and I could wheedle one of our mothers into transporting us the three miles or so to play together at her home.

Farm families didn't have much time for socializing, and Sundays provided the only real opportunities to get together with other family members. As a result, all of my other girl playmates besides Alice Ann were my cousins on Dad's side of the family: Betty Marie Neal, who was two years older than I, and Mary Marchino, who was one year younger.

Dad's oldest sister, my aunt Midah Neal, and her family lived on a farm, called a sand farm because of the sandiness of the soil, off Old Decker Road, about five miles from our house. The back side of the farm adjoined my McCormick grandparents' farm, named Rose Hill Farm because of the rambler roses that grew on the banks of the lane leading to the house. Aunt Dorothy Marchino, Dad's youngest sister, and her family lived farther away, maybe ten miles, toward Fritchton, a tiny town with a twelve-grade school and not much more.

Life on the farm may have been pretty idyllic for Eddie and me, but it was much less so for our parents. The year before I was born, my dad had taken the position of office manager/secretary treasurer of the Knox County Corn-Hog Association, one of the government's farmer-assistance programs. Although the Depression hadn't hit our little farm community as hard as it had so many other places in the Midwest, any extra income was more than welcome and enabled our parents to keep their heads above water. It wasn't easy, however, because he still had a good part of the farm work to do in the mornings and evenings. Meantime, Mother was left during the day to run the farm and take care of the home and family more or less by herself. I'm sure she little suspected that before long Dad's town job would ultimately take him not only away from Vincennes, but as far as the nation's capital.

By the mid-1930s, the country was beginning to recover from the Great Depression. President Franklin Delano Roosevelt had brought forth a number of national programs to get people back to work in the cities, to help farmers increase production, and to stimulate the economy.

By 1934 the population of the United States was creeping past one hundred twenty-six million. People had a little money to spend because jobs were more plentiful than in the previous four years. Prohibition had been repealed, and by the end of that year several notorious outlaws and gangsters — "Pretty Boy" Floyd, "Baby Face" Nelson, John Dillinger, and Bonnie and Clyde — all had been done in by various law enforcement teams. Optimism picked up as people's lives moved on to better times, and numerous new products hit the market with brand names such as Wheaties, Heinz, Frigidaire, and Maxwell House, names that are still famous today. Newspapers cost only two or three cents each and you could mail a letter with a three-cent postage stamp.

Sports were just as popular then as they are now. In 1934, the St. Louis Cardinals won the World Series, and the New York Giants were the pro football champs. Bill Cummings came in first at the Indianapolis 500 (at a rip-roaring 104.863 mph); Wyoming took the NCAA basketball championship and Minnesota held the title for college football. Jockey Mack Garner rode Cavalcade to win the Run for the Roses at the Kentucky Derby. To top it all off, legendary female athlete Babe Didrickson pitched a scoreless inning for the Philadelphia Athletics in an exhibition game against the Brooklyn Dodgers.

*The Princess — at only twenty-
one months of age, I was already
developing a sense of style and
flair.*

*Strutsie at age three, all dressed up and rarin'
to go.*

My brother Jim, (right rear) literally was someone to look up to as he towered over (from left) Eddie, Donnie, and me. In fact, as seen in this family photo, by the time he was fifteen, he already was as tall as Dad.

The family homestead.

CHAPTER 2

The Key to My Frontier
Vincennes' Role in the
Nation's and My Growth

By the time my father's great-great-grandfather moved to Knox County around 1800, Vincennes was already an old and well-established community.

We weren't taught Indiana history in school, so when I was a child I never even considered the story of the area where I grew up, much less its value. As an adult, however, I've come to realize that the history and culture that surrounds you as you mature become an integral part of you.

Briefly, Vincennes, in fact, is the oldest city in the state of Indiana, founded officially in 1732 when François-Marie Bissot, Sieur de Vincennes, built an outpost at a strategic point on the banks of the Ouabache River — known today as the Wabash. Some current historians claim that French traders had settled at the site as early as 1680. It may have seemed an unlikely place for the French to dwell, but the proximity of the Wabash and White rivers and the trapping opportunities they offered drew a few hearty souls from Canada in the 1700s to seek their fortunes. The area was also populated by Indians from the Piankeshaw tribe, who lived peacefully near the small white population, until their expulsion in 1804. In the historical novel *Alice of Old Vincennes*, author Maurice Thompson describes a queer little town with its log dwellings, the rude fort, and the inhabitant blend of traders, soldiers, and woodsmen.

Vincennes thrived and grew. All goods and communication to and from the fledgling city came by boat either from New Orleans, the posts (as the river towns were called) along the northern banks of the Wabash, or from as far north as Detroit.

Father Pierre Gibault came to Vincennes in the mid-1770s to help establish the Catholic religion in the area. (A Vincennes street is named for him, as well as one for Tecumseh, the famous Shawnee Indian chief.) Gibault was a major player during the Revolutionary War when he helped form a consolidation of the French and American armies against the British. Much of the French influence remains to this day. Historical aspects of Vincennes' French origination exist in names of streets (Dubois and Lafayette, for example); the town's layout, which, in typical French tradition, starts from the river; and the dominance of Catholic churches, one of them being the beautiful Old Cathedral, the oldest church in Indiana.

Vincennes was the setting in 1779 when Colonel George Rogers Clark and his troops defeated the British forces at the pivotal Battle of Fort Sackville, which effectively doubled the size of the original thirteen colonies and moved the new nation's western frontier from the Allegheny Mountains to the Mississippi. His actions made Clark a national hero who now stands recognized for all time by the beautiful George Rogers Clark Memorial, located majestically on the banks of the Wabash River in Vincennes and dedicated by President Franklin D. Roosevelt in 1936 as a national memorial. My family and I attended the dedication, and while I was much too young to recall any of it, my mother related that my baby brother, Eddie, fidgeting as infants will, lost one of his booties in the events of that momentous day.

Vincennes has been described as one of the most cosmopolitan cities in the nation because of the succession of flags flown there. First was the brown Indian banner with its feather, cross and turtle; next came the white French flag with three blue fleurs-de-lis, which in turn was replaced by the Madame Godare home-stitched, red-and-green-striped Northwest flag. The yellow Spanish flag flew briefly in 1763 when the French king, foreseeing his country's defeat in the French and Indian War, ceded the territory to his cousin, the king of Spain. The British demanded and received the territory that same year at the Treaty of Paris and unfurled the red, white, and blue Union Jack. Finally, the American flag of red and white stripes with thirteen white stars in a circle on a corner field of blue was hoisted over the fort when Clark and his "Long Knives" recaptured the fort in 1779.

William Henry Harrison governed the territory from 1801 to 1813 from his estate, named Grouseland, where he built the first brick mansion in southern Indiana, a structure that still stands. Grouseland is noted on the Vincennes Historical Tour, and when I visit the city, I love driving past to see the magnificent old home, located on Sixth Street. He negotiated the Treaty of Fort Wayne in 1809, in which the Delaware, Miami, Potawatomi, and Eel River Indians ceded about three million acres of land, greatly angering Tecumseh, the Shawnee leader. Following a bitter confrontation with Tecumseh on the lawn at Grouseland, Harrison and his militia marched on Prophetstown, a village built by Tecumseh's brother, the Prophet. The Prophet and his warriors launched a surprise dawn attack on Harrison's troops, who then counterattacked in the legendary Battle of Tippecanoe, earning Harrison the nickname of "Old Tip."

Harrison was elected the ninth president of the United States in 1841, but held the office for only one month before dying of pneumonia at the age of sixty-seven. His grandson, Benjamin Harrison, became the twenty-third president of the United States, and the only one ever elected from Indiana. I'm proud of this heritage and the people who affirmed the importance of my childhood home.

⁂

The Revolutionary War was over and the young nation was experiencing growing pains. The east was becoming too crowded and too limited for the tastes of those with the pioneering spirit. Thus, drawn by the lure of the open spaces and fertile lands west of the Alleghenies, a migration toward the Northwest Territory began for those seeking to find their fortunes and establish new roots. Among those pioneers was my great-great-great-grandfather, George McCormick.

George McCormick was a descendant of James McCormick, who

had emigrated from Scotland to Northern Ireland in the late 1600s due to religious persecution. James became a Protestant hero at the Battle of the Boyne, defending their stronghold of Londonderry. (He was memorialized in a Londonderry church window and was given a coat of arms featuring a fist clutching a spear.)

James' two sons, Hugh and Thomas, came to America in 1735 and settled in Pennsylvania, near Harrisburg. My ancestry flows from Thomas (1702–1762) through his son, Hugh (1735–1799) and that Hugh's son, George (1771–1839).

The McCormick family made a strong and lasting imprint on the Midwest. Another of my ancestor Hugh's sons, Robert, settled in Virginia in 1779. Among his descendants are Colonel Robert McCormick, who owned the *Chicago Tribune*, and Cyrus McCormick, the inventor of the first mechanical reaper. Son George, meanwhile, moved farther west to Kentucky, where, by 1798, legend has it that his first wife was killed by Indians. After that, George, along with his widowed sister and her small son, left Kentucky via the old Buffalo Trace from Louisville with all their goods — household effects and a kit of blacksmith tools — carried in creels on the backs of beasts of burden. (A buffalo trace was a wide path made by migrations of buffalo, with their heavy bodies and comparatively small feet.)

The exact date of George's and his sister's arrival in Vincennes isn't exactly known, but it was sometime around 1800. The population of the city then was around 714. (By 1810, more than twenty-four thousand souls called Indiana their home.) George met and married Susannah McClure, the daughter of John McClure, a veteran of the Revolutionary War and also one of the first settlers in the area. At the time George and Susannah's first son, Adam, was born on December 2, 1802, Vincennes had one church and two blacksmith shops, one of which belonged to George McCormick.

George and Susannah had five more children, the youngest, Edward Schuler (called "Schuler"), born in 1818. Schuler drove a stage for a man named Samuel Emison, and in time had a freight line of his own. He married Mary Ann "Polly" Price in 1838. The couple set up housekeeping on a farm in Johnson Township in Knox County and had six children, one of whom was John, my great-grandfather, born in 1842.

Farming has always been a labor-intensive endeavor, requiring as many working hands as possible. In the days before mechanized farming, the work was grueling and all the children of a farm family were expected to lend a hand, sometimes taking up some pretty heavy responsibilities as soon as they were able to walk and understand instructions. Young John had to assume the role of head of the house and the farm, however, when Schuler McCormick died of pneumonia in 1857, when John was only fifteen. In 1863, during the Civil War, he took up arms and served with the 118th Indiana Infantry in General Burnside's campaign around Knoxville, Tennessee. He wanted to re-enlist after his six-month period of service ended, but his family persuaded him that their need for him at home outweighed that of the army. As his sister Mary described it: "Ma and Cook and I had to shed some tears, and he decided to stay and put out the crops."

John thus returned to the farm and remained there, helping his mother, until he was twenty-eight years old. Around that time he met Sarah Smithmeier, whose family had emigrated from Germany in 1819, and married her on January 4, 1870. The couple had twelve children, the oldest being my grandfather, born in late 1870 and named John Edward, but called "Ed" or "J. E." to more easily distinguish him from his father. Two sisters died in infancy, and one brother, Clarence, also died young, at age sixteen.

The senior John was a threshing machine operator and was the first in Knox County to own a traction machine. He was also service-minded toward his community, and held the post of deputy assessor of Johnson Township for several years. In 1902, he was badly injured in a horse-and-wagon accident, and complications from internal injuries resulted in his death two years later, in 1904, at the age of sixty-two. His widow left the farm and moved to Vincennes, where she lived until her death in 1915.

Minerva "Minnie" Rodarmel (one of thirteen children in her family) became Ed's bride on December 12, 1894. They had two daughters, Midah, born in 1897, and Mildred, born in 1899, when a boy finally arrived on March 26, 1902 — Clarence James McCormick, my dad. The family lived at that time on a rented farm about eight miles south of Vincennes near the Wabash River, where Ed not only farmed but also continued his father's wheat threshing operation with his brothers. Fish from the nearby river often supplemented the family's diet.

The turn of the century brought many changes to rural Indiana, several of them making life easier for farmers. Mail was at last delivered to the farmsteads with the advent of Rural Free Delivery (RFD) in 1900. Even more dramatic was the first stringing of telephone lines through the countryside in 1903, making Alexander Graham Bell's invention, the telephone, patented in 1878, a standard feature in many farm homes. Farmers supplied their own posts.

Ed McCormick continued to be a tenant farmer until 1909, at which time he bought a 180-acre farm just off Old Decker Road and about eight miles from Vincennes. By that time, the family had grown to include John, Dorothy, and Earl. The house was heated by coal and wood stoves, and a large steel range with a six-gallon reservoir was used for cooking and to heat the kitchen. Light was provided by coal oil lamps and lanterns, and a windmill powered the water supply. Because there was no refrigeration in the house, Ed built a special tight oak box about fifteen feet long and put it in the milk house. Water piped from the windmill flowed through the box to cool the crocks of milk and out into the watering trough for the livestock. Along with cattle, hogs, and chickens, Ed and Minnie also raised corn, wheat, fruit, and garden products. This farm would be Ed and Minnie's home for the rest of their lives.

The house itself was rather large. A master bedroom with a small dressing room, a sitting room, a parlor, a dining room, a large country kitchen, and a pantry occupied the first floor. The children's bedrooms were upstairs. Besides the front and back porches, the house also had an enclosed side porch that held Ed's big desk, where he kept his meticulous ledgers.

Grandpa Ed McCormick was an enterprising farmer, and he hired out his threshing machine to farmers throughout the county. He also had an avid fascination for horticulture, and he was able to profit from this hobby with a flourishing peach orchard located on the farm. He loved to experiment with grafting fruit trees and nut trees, sometimes producing some rather strange combinations. One time he had three varieties of apples growing on the same tree. In addition to peaches and apples, he grew plums, raspberries, strawberries, gooseberries, blueberries, cherries, and watermelons. He also had a passion for roses, and planted so many on the banks of the land leading to the house that the property became known as "Rose Hill Farm."

In 1909, the one-room grade school, called the Mail School, was close enough for the children to walk to school. One teacher taught all eight grades.

When my aunt Midah finished eighth grade, she traveled to Decker to take the state-required examination for graduation. She passed, but continuing on to high school presented somewhat of a problem. Aunt Midah wrote about this in her memoirs in 1979:

> In those days, not everyone graduated from eighth grade and fewer still went ahead to high school. One reason for this was the need of farmers for their sons to help on the farm. So much more help was needed to operate horse-drawn machinery and so many more farmers were needed to feed the nation when crops produced only low yields.
>
> Another reason fewer attended high school was that there was no public transportation for the pupils. My father solved this problem by sending me to live in the home of my Grandmother McCormick [in] Vincennes. . . .
>
> In our class of the Vincennes High School in 1910, there were only fifty freshmen.

By the following year, Decker had received its credit as a commissioned high school and Midah began her sophomore year there, traveling back and forth by a buggy pulled by her horse, Lou. When my dad began high school he also got there by horse and buggy, but soon after, bus service was begun to transport students to Decker High.

Six of the McCormick children graduated from Decker High School. (John had suffered a serious illness as an infant that left him learning impaired.) Seven students were in Midah's graduating class, Decker High's first, in 1914. That same year Grandpa Ed bought his first automobile, a hand-cranked Ford with a decorative brass band across the front radiator. It enabled the family to more easily make the five-mile trips to attend Sunday services at Trinity Methodist.

That was a good thing for my Grandma McCormick, who was very service-minded, and a dedicated church-goer who taught Sunday school at Trinity for more than thirty years. Grandma was also as creative in her own areas of interest as her husband was in horticulture. She was the first person in Knox County to have a home sewing machine and women would come from miles around to use it. Grandma was a talented seamstress with a flair for designing and making patterns for clothes, as well as constructing them. Her creativity was evident, too, in the unusual gifts she made for her family, such as a little pillowcase with a silver dollar tucked inside as a surprise.

Aunt Midah wanted to be a public school teacher, and after discussing it with her father, it was decided that she would attend Vincennes University. Grandpa McCormick loaned her the forty-two-dollar tuition fee, and in the fall of 1914 she again went to live with her grandmother, which enabled her to walk to her classes. Midah was sixteen at the time, and only seventy-five students comprised the university's enrollment.

Only two semesters of study were required to be a teacher then. Midah took the examination for her teacher's license but didn't pass the first two times. Like the rest of her family, however, she was not a quitter, and on her third attempt she passed and received her license to teach in any township in Knox County. In the fall of 1915, at the age of seventeen, Midah began her teaching career at School Number 9, a small school in Decker. She taught all eight grades, and among her pupils was thirteen-year-old Emma Bobe, who seven years later would become the wife of Midah's younger brother Clarence.

In the early part of the twentieth century, farm life didn't leave much time for socializing, and church activities were the best way for people to get together with others.

The McCormicks had always been active at Trinity Methodist, and Clarence was no exception. By seventh grade, he was already one of the driving forces in the Epworth League, the Methodist Church's youth movement. Young Emma Bobe and her siblings also attended League meetings, and Emma caught Clarence's eye almost immediately. Captivated by Emma's blond, blue-eyed good looks and her dimpled smile, Clarence soon was giving her rides home in his horse-drawn buggy after League meetings. She lived only about a mile from the church, which was fortunate for Clarence's patient sisters, who were left waiting at the church, cooling their heels and watching the sun go down, until he returned to take them home.

As innocent as walks together on Sunday afternoons and buggy rides after Epworth League meetings sound, my grandfather Bobe, Emma's father, believed that his daughter and her beau were too young for such carryings-on.

August Bobe, my mother's father, was the product of an old-world upbringing. His parents, Heinrich and Wilhelmina Held Bobe, immigrated to New Orleans from Prussia, a part of northern Germany on the Baltic Sea, in 1852. Their first child was born that year, perhaps on the ocean voyage to the U.S. In all, Heinrich and Wilhelmina had nine children. My grandfather, August, born in 1867, was the sixth.

My great-grandparents eventually brought their family north to Indiana and settled in Knox County, possibly following other relatives. Knox County had a large contingent of Germans and among them was a young woman named Sophia Vollmer. She was the seventh of eleven children in her family, and in 1891, at the age of twenty-five, she married August Bobe.

August and Sophia settled on a farm about four miles east of Vincennes, on lower Hart Street Road. They had nine children, the youngest a boy named Robert, born in 1909. That birth took its toll on Sophia, and not long afterward, at the age of forty-three, she died. Their eldest daughter, seventeen-year-old Lilly, had always helped with the younger children, but now she became the sole surrogate mother for the brood: Clarence, age fifteen; Selma, fourteen; Oscar, twelve; Helen, ten; Emma, seven; Gilbert, six; and Raymond, four. The little baby was more than Lilly could handle, so three-month-old Robert was taken and raised by August's brother John and his wife, Lou.

The family remained on the farm. My grandfather August was a dairyman with a herd of twenty-some cows. These were milked by hand, after which the milk was delivered in five-gallon cans to customers in Vincennes by horse and wagon. August also did custom threshing, raised melons, and was a "trader." He was a bit of a pack-rat, fond of collecting all sorts of things, and the area near the barns was always full of his "treasures." He was also somewhat of a dare-devil, which more or less led to his death in 1932. The *Vincennes Sun-Commercial* printed the following account of his demise on November 16 of that year:

> *Mr. Bobe was doing some work on a fence in the barn lot three weeks ago last Monday when the enraged bull attacked him. He drove it off after the first attack and gave no further attention to the animal until it again attacked him. His daughter, Miss Lilly Bobe, heard her father's cries for help and with their large shepherd dog ran to his rescue. The dog drove off the bull, which was pawing at the prostrate farmer, and he was dragged from the lot. Although Mr. Bobe suffered painful bruises about the chest, his condition was not believed serious until complications developed.*

He died three weeks later. He was age 65 years, eight months, and 28 days and his advancing age was against him in the hopeless battle for recovery.

As his eldest grandchildren recalled, August Bobe was a strict disciplinarian, especially with his sons. Despite that, he had a great sense of humor and loved to tease. He also had a few eccentricities, such as wearing long underwear all year round and bathing in the icy water of the tank used for chilling the milk crocks.

All of the Bobe children, like most farm children then, learned the rigors of hard work at an early age. By the time they were nine or ten, the girls were responsible for milking the cows both morning and evening. Lilly, as the eldest, ran the household.

The four girls shared one of the two bedrooms in the house, and the younger children slept in their parents' bedroom. The older boys slept in the "shack," a small house behind the main house where the hired men slept. The house also contained a living room, a dining room, and a kitchen with a table large enough for all of the family plus whatever extra hands were working at the time. A side porch was used for laundry and other chores during warm weather. The house, barns, and outbuildings were set back about a quarter of a mile or so from the gravel road. Pastures for the milk cows surrounded the back buildings, and flower beds, which the girls loved tending, adorned the front yard near the house. There was, of course, the ever-present and ever-necessary vegetable garden.

Little Emma was a lovely child with her golden blond hair, blue eyes, and dimples. She grew up in the heart of a fun-loving family that enjoyed life, despite the loss of their mother. The siblings had affectionate nicknames for each other, some imaginative, some not so. Lilly was called Lil, Clarence was Cat, Selma was Sam, and Oscar was Slick. Then there was Runt (Helen), Em (Emma), Gib (Gilbert), and Ray (Raymond). Robert, the baby of the family, was always simply "Robert," probably because he didn't grow up with the rest of them. They were a close-knit group that knew the importance of supporting and taking care of each other. A favorite story was about Gib when he was a mischievous youngster and fell out of a tree, breaking his arm. Lilly was alarmed, but Gib shrugged his sister's concerns off. "It *tould*'ve been worse," he proclaimed, unperturbed. "It *tould*'ve been my neck!"

School Number 9 was about a half-mile from the Bobe home, and all of the children graduated from the eighth grade there. Lessons were rigorous, requiring a lot of memorization of poetry, as well as basic skills in math, grammar, geography, and history. The girls also learned home crafts, such as sewing and needlework, especially embroidery and crocheting. Further education in high school, however, was not too realistic an option, much less going to college. Helen, the third daughter, went on to high school, then to Vincennes University. The "baby," Robert, because he was raised as an only child by his aunt and uncle, was able to not only graduate from high school, but also went to college and to medical school in St. Louis.

My mother's formal education ended at eighth grade. She was, however, a very intelligent girl who had an aptitude and talent for music, one of the great joys of her life, and her father saw to it that she was able to take piano lessons in Vincennes. Her brother Ray had a lovely voice and often sang solos at church, frequently with Emma as his accompanist. Emma may have lacked some of the social skills associated with attending high school, but her abbreviated education never held her back, nor deterred her from having a full life.

As a young adult, my mother experienced the tragedy of the loss of her older sister Selma, who suffered a ruptured appendix and died of peritonitis in 1926 at the age of thirty. Six years later, her father died, and another six years after that, in 1938, her youngest brother, Robert, died of heart disease.

All of the surviving siblings eventually married (except Lilly) and lived in the Vincennes area all of their lives. The family remained close, and family reunions at Gregg Park in Vincennes were always an event to look forward to. Tables were piled high with tempting food, and because they enjoyed a good time together, the mood was always lively. The Bobe siblings and their families would gather at the park's shelter house right after church on Sunday (early family arrivals secured the shelter house for us), put paper coverings on the tables, and did whatever else was necessary to prepare for the forthcoming food baskets.

The assortment of food each lady brought — country cooking at its very best! — was truly the stuff of which memories are made: fried chicken, slaw, sliced tomatoes, potato salad, and assorted meat and vegetable dishes. Then there were the desserts. Oh, my! How good they were! We had fruit cobblers, cream pies (my Aunt Edna made the world's best coconut, banana, and chocolate cream pies), cookies, and a variety of cakes.

After I married and had my own family, whenever we came to the reunions my contribution was a cake that in time I called "Reunion Cake." The platter is likely to be licked clean when this cake is gone — even the crumbs are good!

Reunion Cake

FOR THE CAKE:

¼ pound chopped dates	1 egg
1 teaspoon baking soda	1 teaspoon vanilla
1 cup boiling water	1 ½ cups all-purpose flour
1 cup sugar	1 teaspoon salt
½ cup shortening	

FOR THE TOPPING:

½ cup brown sugar	½ cup chopped pecans
3 tablespoons cream	½ cup coconut
3 tablespoons butter	

Combine the dates and baking soda in a small bowl. Pour the boiling water over the mixture and set aside while combining the other ingredients.

In a large mixing bowl, combine the sugar and shortening and cream until fluffy. Add the egg and vanilla and beat until combined. Add the dry ingredients alternately with the dates and soda mixture. Pour into a greased and floured 9-by-13-inch pan. Bake for 45 minutes at 350 degrees.

Meanwhile, combine the topping ingredients. When cake is done, and while still hot, sprinkle the topping mixture over it. Place cake under the broiler just until the topping becomes bubbly.

Good times were had by all at the reunions. The adults passed the time visiting with each other and the children played on the swings and teeter-totters until it was time for naps (for both young and old). At the end of the day, the remains of the food and the dirty dishes were gathered up. Good-byes were mixed with comments of "See you all next year," when, the good Lord willing, everyone would meet again. It wasn't that the family didn't see each other in between reunions, because they did, but there was something special in having everyone together at once to take pictures and marvel at how the children had grown. The memories those reunions created are among the most precious ones I have.

As time went by, the romance between my parents blossomed and grew while my dad finished high school, attended Vincennes University and then State Normal (now Indiana State University), where he studied to be a teacher. He played basketball on the State Normal team, and in an old newspaper clipping was called "the hot-shot from Vincennes." His coach was Birch Bayh, father of Birch Bayh, Jr., the former U.S. senator from Indiana, and the grandfather of Indiana's former governor and now senator, Evan Bayh.

In the meantime, Emma remained in the family home with her father and siblings, doing her part to help care for the house and the farm.

After leaving State Normal in 1922 at age twenty, Dad took a teaching position at Decker High School. There he taught botany and agriculture and was also the basketball coach. He worked hard and saved as much as he could so he could marry his sweetheart and begin a new life. On the warm summer afternoon of August 28, 1923, eight years after they began their courtship, Clarence McCormick took Emma Bobe as his bride. They both were twenty-one years old.

Mother's parents, August and Sophie Vollmer Bobe.

My grandfather Bobe's dairy delivered milk in the Vincennes area in wagons such as this.

Dad's parents, Ed and Minnie Rodarmel McCormick.

My mother's fresh loveliness at age sixteen drew the eyes of young men, and her father was protective of her . . .

But the handsome young basketball player, Clarence McCormick, was hard to resist, and won her heart and her father's approval.

In time, they became sweethearts . . . then husband and wife.

CHAPTER 3

An Untraditional Life
on Our Farm

My father, at a young age, knew that hard work was a key to success, but that there was much more to it than that. He was a visionary who had a plan for his family, his farm, and his future, and he was willing to take calculated risks in order to secure his dreams. He had learned that his goals would be realized only if he used his God-given talents creatively and was willing to put his utmost efforts behind them. That was a gift he passed on to his children, and one that has always served all of us well.

It was also in his young adulthood that my dad established a lifelong pattern of always working in multiples — multitasking, you might say — holding at least two jobs, serving in two or more leadership roles in organizations, and so on, another trait that all of his children would emulate in their turn. In retrospect, it's easy to understand what compelled him to work as hard as he did. His dreams kept him motivated. So did his faith, which never wavered, even when his life took unexpected turns.

After my parents' marriage they settled on a rented farm a few miles from Decker, where Dad continued to teach at the high school for another three years, until 1926. The town of Decker in the early part of the century was a lively little community of about four hundred. It was about a quarter of a mile from the White River, and was situated on the C&EI Railroad, which gave it the double advantage of both river and railroad transportation for people as well as the shipping and receiving of goods.

Much of the land around Decker was sandy loam, which produced bumper crops of melons and berries, as well as thriving orchards, all of which were a prime source of employment and income for those who lived in the area.

Despite the fact that Decker's streets were unpaved, and that the town had no sewers, no water system, and no electricity or street-lights, it did boast five churches, a Farmer and Merchant's Bank, four general stores, a post office, a depot, and four saloons, which were shut down during Prohibition. A town marshal maintained the peace.

When the high school was built, it became the heart of the community. The school's successful basketball team was a great source of pride, and when Decker High built one of the first lighted baseball fields in southern Indiana, fans came from far and wide to see such notable Big League stars as Gil Hodges and Don Liddle play there.

Clarence and Emma McCormick continued tenant farming for a few more years, and finally, around 1929, they were able to move to a farm that in time would become their own. By then they had one son, Jimmie, born in 1925. Things seemed promising, then the stock market crash of 1929 brought the Great Depression, and the future of many farms became uncertain. Farmers struggled just to make ends meet and keep their farms; actually making any money from them was a completely different issue.

During the years before there was much in the way of gaso-line-run machinery farming was grueling. Dad had a team of mules that was used for plowing, planting, and harvesting, and for pulling the manure spreader over the fields. The mules required a person to direct them, however, and that for the most part fell to my broth-er Jim, who learned to drive the team by the time he was only six years old.

Farms were pretty much self-sustaining entities in those days, and most of the goods produced on the farm were consumed either by the family or the animals. The vegetable garden abounded with long rows of tomatoes, potatoes, green beans, peas, cabbages, leaf lettuce, radishes, beets, and carrots, providing produce for canning, storing, or eating fresh. Sliced tomatoes were featured at almost every meal during the summer, but plenty were available for canning as juice or whole, which were delicious eaten cold from the jar.

The fruit trees on the farm produced apples and red cherries, which made the most delicious pies. The apples were used for canning applesauce, which often was served as a light dessert. Peaches came from my grandfather McCormick's farm, as well as strawberries and gooseberries. Blackberries grew wild in the ravines around the countryside that we called "hollers," and those too were picked during the month of June to fill the fruit jars for winter consumption.

We didn't grow cantaloupes and watermelons, because they required sandy soil that we didn't have on our farm, but many of our neighbors had fields of them, so we would purchase them in July and August. They were a wonderfully refreshing treat! Dad absolutely loved to crack open a fresh watermelon and eat a chunk of it while the juice dripped on the ground. Seeing how far he could spit the seeds was a part of the process, of course.

Every spring, Mother had a "special project": the raising of baby chicks. Off she would go to Vincennes to buy them, and return with five hundred of the little golden fuzz balls in big flat boxes that had holes in the sides for ventilation. The boxes were carefully emptied inside the smallest of our three chicken houses, called the brooder house. The brooder house had heaters that kept the chicks warm at night, and she would fill their troughs with fresh water and food twice a day. Once the chicks were old enough to go outside, she would open the small doors on the side of the building so they could get fresh air and exercise. The chicks' yard was alternated with the garden space, and their droppings provided fertilizer for the next year's garden. They remained in their own space through the summer, until they were a couple of pounds in weight. Mother sold some of them, and the rest of them spent their adulthood in the big chicken houses. Of course, the flock would be somewhat depleted now and then as the unlucky ones showed up on the table as fried chicken dinners. The survivors were revenue producers. The cash Mother used for household purchases came mostly from her chicken business. She sold eggs to the hatchery in Vincennes year round. Who knows, maybe some of her own eggs became the baby chicks she raised.

Our farm was truly a business, and almost everything we grew was for the purpose of generating income to keep the business going. In addition to chickens, our livestock included milk cows, feeder cows, hogs, and sheep, and tending to all these animals required several hours' work every morning and evening — seven days a week and holidays. Milk, cream, and butter came from the milk cows, and the feeder cows and hogs provided beef and pork. The feeder cows and hogs were sold when they reached maturity, and some of the income from them was used to purchase calves and pigs to start the cycle again. Wool was shorn from the sheep, stuffed into big bags and delivered to market for sale.

We also raised grain crops for sale — corn, wheat, oats, and soybeans. Some of the corn we kept and made into silage used to feed the livestock. The rest of the grain crops were stored in grain bins and silos for later delivery to the market.

The farm did well considering the harshness of the times, but it still was pretty much a break-even enterprise, and almost every penny was committed to paying bills or purchasing livestock, seed grain for planting, fertilizer, tools, equipment, and maintenance. Because of that, my dad always had a job in addition to farming. This was especially important in the 1930s, while the country struggled to recover from the Depression. Dad had always been an active participant in local affairs, but I believe the Depression was the catalyst for the great things he would accomplish later. He was both college-educated and ambitious, and he used those to his best advantage. In 1933, he was offered a position as the office manager/secretary-treasurer of the Knox County Corn-Hog Association, one of the government's farmer-assistance programs. Dad's schedule required unbelievably long hours; he had to be up before dawn to do farm chores, clean up and dress in suit and tie and drive to Vincennes for his office job, then don his work clothes again when he got home at the end of the day to complete the evening chores. I doubt that he ever complained, though. He saw it as an opportunity to combine his interest in farming with a salary and career advancement, however, and he accepted the job. This was the schedule he was keeping when I was born in 1934.

Living in the little rural community near Vincennes, Mother and Dad might not have been aware that Adolph Hitler was elected president of Germany in 1933, or that Shirley Temple was making her first movie. Those things had no effect on their lives at that time. I'm sure they didn't realize that, according to national statistics, their life expectancy was only 59.7 years. They may not have been very interested in the popular big bands and singers of the day: Benny Goodman, Duke Ellington, Rudy Vallee, Bing Crosby, or Eddy Duchin, who were recording hit tunes such as "Moon Glow," "Cocktails for Two," "Everything I Have Is Yours," "June in January," and "Let's Fall in Love" — all of which still are being played and even recorded yet today.

My parents didn't spend their hard-earned cash on such necessities as milk (which sold for forty-two cents per gallon), eggs (seventeen cents per dozen), or hamburger (twelve cents per pound), because they produced these on the farm. They did buy sugar (fifty-nine cents for ten pounds) because it was needed for canning fruits, and purchased gasoline (ten cents per gallon) because they owned an automobile. But the car was neither a Hudson nor a Packard (each of which cost approximately six hundred and twenty-five dollars). Theirs was a less-expensive Ford.

They probably went to an occasional movie, which then was a bargain at only twenty-five cents a ticket. Some of the hits in 1934 were *The Thin Man, The Gay Divorcee,* and the Academy Award-winner, *It Happened One Night.* (Those three titles alone could be another movie!) Time was as scarce as cash was, however, and most likely my parents' entertainment was limited to Sunday dinners with relatives after attending Sunday school and church services at Trinity Methodist. The church was only a couple of miles from our home, and we attended Sunday school and church every Sunday from nine-thirty a.m. until noon. Mother's musical talents were well used there, where she was the church pianist and later, the organist.

My own special entertainment on summer Sundays when I was a preschooler was licking the paddle on the ice cream freezer after Dad finished cranking it. Homemade ice cream was a special treat to go along with Mother's wonderful cakes. Unless it was a birthday, the cake was probably sponge cake served with fresh strawberries, or it might have been a Lady Baltimore cake that Mother's sister Helen liked to make. For birthdays, only angel food cake would do. Mother used the recipe on the Swans Down Cake Flour box exclusively for many years, until she discovered Betty Crocker's cake mixes. But those cakes were never as good as her made-from-scratch specialties.

Sponge Cake

This cake was our favorite base for strawberry shortcake. If you reduce the eggs to three, you can use it to make the pineapple upside-down cake that's featured later in this book.

4 eggs, separated

1 cup sugar

¼ cup water

1 cup flour

1 slightly heaping teaspoon baking powder

Beat whites until stiff; set aside. Beat yolks until lemon-colored and thick, and gradually add the sugar. Add liquid and dry ingredients alternately. Pour into an ungreased 9-by-12-inch pan or a tube pan. Bake at 350 degrees until the top springs back when lightly touched, approximately 45 minutes.

Lady Baltimore Cake

BEAT UNTIL STIFF:

6 egg whites with ¼ teaspoon cream of tartar

SIFT TOGETHER 3 TIMES:

2 ½ cups cake flour

¼ teaspoon salt

3 teaspoons baking powder

ROLL IN FLOUR:

½ cup chopped nuts

18 maraschino cherries, drained and chopped fine

COMBINE:

¼ cup reserved cherry juice

½ cup milk

1 teaspoon vanilla

Combine all ingredients, folding in beaten egg whites last. Bake at 350 degrees in a greased 9 ½-by-13 ½-inch pan for 30 minutes or until done.

Angel Food Cake

MEASURE AND SIFT TOGETHER **3** TIMES:

1 cup cake flour

⅞ cup (¾ cup + 2 tablespoons) sugar

MEASURE INTO LARGE MIXING BOWL:

1 ½ cups egg whites, at room temperature

1 1½ teaspoons cream of tartar

¼ teaspoon salt

1 ½ teaspoons vanilla

½ teaspoon almond extract

¾ cup sugar

With a wire whisk, beat egg whites just until frothy. Add the cream of tartar and salt and beat until well blended. Gradually add the sugar, 2 tablespoons at a time, beating about 10 seconds after each addition. When the sugar is well incorporated, add the vanilla and almond extract and continue beating until the mixture holds stiff straight peaks when the whisk is gently lifted out. (This requires a lot of beating.)

Place flour/sugar mixture in sifter and sift about 3 tablespoons over the entire surface of meringue at a time, using about 8 or 10 complete folding strokes and turning the bowl a quarter of a turn with each stroke. Repeat this process until all the flour and sugar is folded in. Pour the batter carefully into an ungreased 10-inch tube pan. Cut carefully through the batter five or six times with a knife or spatula to break large air bubbles. Bake at 350 degrees 35-45 minutes. Remove from oven and immediately invert the pan. Leave the cake upside-down in the pan until completely cooled.

Emma's Cream Icing

This is wonderful on cakes and cookies.

Cook ¾ cup thick sweet cream and 1 cup sugar to a soft ball stage (232 to 234 degrees). Cool to 110 degrees. Add 1 teaspoon vanilla. Beat the mixture until well blended and smooth.

I loved watching Mother assemble the utensils and ingredients for the special "Birthday Angel Food Cake." She used a big ceramic bowl, white on the inside and a pretty green on the outside, about fourteen inches in diameter and six inches deep. She would carefully crack about a dozen eggs, one by one, on the side of the bowl, separating the whites from the yolks. (The yolks were used later in scrambled eggs.) Mother then would sit down in a kitchen chair and begin to whisk the egg whites with a flat metal beater used only for this purpose.

Once the whites were thick and foamy, she would gradually whisk in the rest of the ingredients until the mixture stood in peaks. Then she would carefully pour the batter into a tube pan that was reserved only for these cakes. With a clean table knife, she'd gently slice through the batter to release air bubbles, give the cake a few taps to further free it of bubbles, then placed the pan on the bottom shelf of the preheated oven.

Oh my! The aroma in the kitchen from the baking was as heavenly as the cake itself!

When Mother deemed the cake to be done, she removed it from the oven and turned the pan upside down to rest on a cup and let it cool completely, which usually took a couple of hours. She'd then slide a long, thin knife around the edges of the pan, turn it upside down, give it a quick, sharp shake, and the beautiful cake would plop onto a cake plate, ready to be frosted with her special cream icing. While she was making the icing, I busied myself with a spoon, scraping out the remaining crust from the cake pan. It was a special treat, and I thought it was the best part of the yummy cake. When Eddie became old enough to know what he was missing, he and I took turns scraping. Candles would be added to the cake just before serving. Maybe the cake wasn't particularly fancy, but it sure was good.

Birthday parties that included anyone other than family were a rarity, so Mother was spared having to dream up themes. I had only two parties when I was a child, the first being when I turned six. The extended family attended — aunts, uncles, cousins, and Grandma and Grandpa McCormick. I don't recall any presents, and there probably weren't any, since we had few toys.

When I turned sixteen, my cousin Alice Ann Osborne gave a surprise party for me in their home's basement, which had been fixed up somewhat. (A basement is different from a cellar, with higher concrete walls and floor. Our cellar was more like a cave — definitely not a party room.) It was a memorable party, in part because it was the first time I had ever played "Spin the Bottle."

Dad evidently was successful in his work with the Knox County Corn-Hog Association in Vincennes, because in 1935 he was offered a new job instructing county officers of the Agricultural Adjustment Administration (another Depression-era government program) on their corn-hog programs. It was an excellent opportunity, but difficult for those of us at home, as it meant his working in an office in Lafayette, Indiana, more than one hundred and forty miles away. Daily commutes were out of the question, of course, and Dad became a weekend farmer.

Since I was only a toddler at the time, I was oblivious to how difficult this situation must have been for Mother. She was by herself with three children, expecting the fourth (Eddie, who was born in 1936). Jimmie was eleven at the time, and he became "the little man" of the family. Fortunately, we also had hired help, and Mother acted as the manager while Dad was gone.

Even with help from her children and hired hands, Mother still had plenty on her hands. Surely farm wives were the original multitaskers. Considering everything they had to do, I have to wonder how there were enough hours in the day. For example, basic housekeeping was much more difficult in those days of heating stoves or coal furnaces in the winter and wide-open windows in the summer. Spring and fall cleaning was essential to remove the accumulated dirt. Curtains were taken down, washed, and put out to dry in the backyard on stretchers, which were wooden frames with short pins protruding around the edge. The curtain edges were secured to the stretchers by pushing them onto the pins. This technique eliminated ironing. The rugs would be rolled up and taken outside on the ground where they would be unrolled and beaten with a big wire beater that looked sort of like a giant spatula. It was quite a workout. No need for farm wives to go to an exercise class! The walls were washed, the windows were cleaned and polished inside and out, floors were scrubbed, and cupboards were emptied, cleaned, and reorganized. This whole process took several days, so it's easy to see why the thorough cleaning was done only twice a year.

The warm months were spent tending the gardens. This meant getting the beds tilled for planting in the spring, weeding with a hoe throughout the entire growing season, harvesting the vegetables, and canning what would be needed for the winter months. Once farm children were old enough to help, which was usually as soon as they were old enough to walk and follow instructions, assisting in the garden often became their first chore. I have many memories of picking peas, green beans, and tomatoes, pulling radishes and carrots, and cutting leaf lettuce and heads of cabbage. If a farm had fruit trees, picking the fruit also fell into the children's jurisdiction. We had a couple of cherry trees near the house, in the chicken yard, and I was posted to them with a ladder, a small metal bucket, and an S-shaped hook. One end of the hook went over the tree limb, while the other end hooked onto the handle of the bucket, which freed up both hands for picking. It was a messy job, and I was usually covered with juice up to my elbows and beyond the whole time I was in the tree. Those trees produced lots of fruit, and I always picked several bucketsful to supply Mother with the necessary amount for her wonderful cherry pies. Little brother Ed was also assigned to pick cherries but somehow always finagled his way out of it.

Most farm women, and especially my mother and her sisters, loved flowers, so they would have an abundance of them. While the vegetables provided food for the body, the colorful blossoms were a feast for the eyes and the soul. Rows of sunny annuals, such as zinnias, marigolds, jewel-like dahlias, and modest daisies grew among the vegetables in the garden. Perennials — brilliant blue irises and fragrant peonies and phlox — grew around the house, accented with dahlias and delicate white baby's breath.

Food on the farm was fresh and plentiful. Until I was about eight years old, all our milk came from our own cows. Buckets of fresh milk were brought from the barn to the back porch, where they were strained to get out whatever debris was there from the milking process. The milk was then poured into one-gallon ceramic crocks which were placed in the refrigerator to chill. After a while, the thick cream would rise to the top to be skimmed off for making butter or whipped cream, or poured onto cereal or home-canned fruit, such as blackberries. One of my favorite childhood treats was to place a piece of homemade white bread in the bottom of a dish, dip home-canned blackberries and juice onto it, and pour thick cream on top. Visions of it still float into my memory every now and then.

Cooking took up a large portion of a farm woman's time. Workdays on a farm were long — literally from dawn to dusk, if not longer — and the labor was grueling. A lot of food was needed to provide the fuel to keep workers going. Farm women cooked a hot breakfast, which was eaten usually after everyone had been up and at work for an hour or so. The main meal of the day was at noon, and often included hired hands at the table as well as family members.

The noon meal during the summer involved much more than just cooking and serving. We spent the morning harvesting vegetables from the garden. The vegetables were cleaned, then peas had to be popped out of their pods, and green beans and asparagus had to be snapped. Along with fresh vegetables, fluffy mashed potatoes were served with hot milk gravy, white bread and homemade butter, and, usually, the crowning centerpiece — crispy fried chicken.

Preparing the chicken also required a lot of work, because our meat was fresh off the hoof, so to speak. First, we'd go out to the chicken yard and grab two or three chickens, tie their legs together with fabric strips, hang them upside down on the clothesline, and whack their heads off with a butcher knife. (Mother was the whacker.) I then took the headless birds to the "production area" in the chicken yard, where I would dip them into buckets of boiling water and pluck the feathers off by hand. The denuded chickens were hauled to the trash barrel, where I would ignite crumpled newspapers and hold the chickens over the flames to loosen the pin feathers. Finally, I delivered them to Mother on the back porch, where she washed them, popped out the pin feathers, cut off the feet, removed the innards, and cut the birds up. (When I married, I didn't know how to cut up a chicken because that had never been my job!) From there it was a trip to the large cast-iron skillets for cooking. We always kept the fat rendered from other foods in a grease jar on the stove, and that was used to fry the chickens, along with some lard from the five-gallon can kept in the cellar. No one uses that kind of fat anymore, which is probably why fried chicken just doesn't taste quite as good these days.

Dessert, usually some sort of pie or cobbler, was requisite, of course. The meal just wouldn't have been complete without it. Sweetened iced tea was the usual beverage, made in a big crock and ladled into a pitcher for pouring. Because sugar was rationed during World War II, Mother used saccharin to sweeten the tea and saved the sugar for her baking.

Supper was probably the lightest meal of the day, usually with just the family members in attendance. Much of the time, our summer suppers consisted of sliced tomatoes, cucumber salad (peeled, thinly sliced cucumbers marinated in a salt/vinegar mixture), fresh cabbage slaw, crispy fried potatoes, some type of meat (maybe leftover fried chicken), and whatever dessert was left over. My contribution to this meal? I was the chief potato peeler, slicer, and fryer.

A favorite breakfast treat for us made only when a hog was butchered was pawnhaus, a Pennsylvania Dutch delicacy, similar to scrapple, made from a hog's head, corn meal, and spices (although I'll bet you'd be hard pressed to find a child nowadays who would even touch it). After cooking, the mixture was poured into loaf pans and refrigerated. It was sliced for breakfast and fried to accompany our eggs, along with liberal servings of homemade catsup poured over the top.

Pawnhaus

Note: This is a recipe you'll just have to "eyeball," because the amount of cornmeal and seasonings used will depend upon the amount of broth and meat you end up with.

Put a hog's head in a large pot. Add enough water to cover by an inch or so and some salt. Bring to a boil, then reduce heat and simmer until the meat is tender. Strain the broth and reserve. When the meat has cooled enough to handle, pick it off the bones and run it through a food grinder.

Bring the broth to a boil in a large pot. Add the meat to the broth and bring to a low boil again. Add cornmeal, a small amount at a time, stirring continuously. Be careful — it will pop. Add just enough cornmeal until the mixture becomes really thick, but not so thick that you can't stir it. Reduce heat to a simmer and continue cooking about 30 minutes or so, stirring continually. Season the mixture with allspice and salt to suit your taste.

When the mixture is cooked, pour it into loaf pans and refrigerate overnight. It will set up as it cools. Once it's ready, slice it and dredge the slices in dry cornmeal and fry to brown.

We had two cast-iron skillets that we always used for frying our foods. One was about fourteen inches in diameter, and the other was twelve inches. The smaller skillet also doubled as the pan for my grand-champion Pineapple Upside-Down Cake.

Pineapple Upside-Down Cake

Prepare the sponge cake recipe found earlier in the book, but use only 3 eggs instead of 4.

Preheat oven to 350 degrees. Place 3 tablespoons butter in an iron skillet, and place the skillet in the oven until the butter is melted. Remove and stir in ½ cup brown sugar. Working quickly so the skillet won't cool off too much, arrange drained canned pineapple rings in a single layer in the butter and sugar mixture and place a maraschino cherry in the center of each ring. Arrange pecan halves around the pineapple rings. Pour the cake batter over the pineapple. Bake for about 45 minutes or until it springs back when lightly touched. Immediately invert the cake onto a cake plate. Let cool.

Bringing up the children was one of the most important factors of farm life, and farm women were always available to lend a hand with schoolwork and 4-H projects. Many of them also were active in their churches and taught Sunday school classes. My mother also played the piano and the organ for services. Needless to say, these women tucked their families in early and went to bed early at night themselves. There was no compulsion in those days to keep children "entertained," and discipline was rarely required. My brothers recall occasional spankings, but I don't remember getting any myself. (Not that I was any better behaved, but I was, after all, the only girl — "The Princess.")

Dad's next career advancement came later in 1936, the year of Ed's birth, when he switched from Agricultural Adjustment Administration to the Extension Service at Purdue University. Actually, the Extension Service was run by the government and Purdue administered it as the land-grant college in the state of Indiana. As an extension supervisor, he traveled the state quite a bit. In that same year, Dad's multitasking skills were put to good use, as he played an instrumental role in starting the Knox County Rural Electrification Administration cooperative, bringing electricity to rural communities.

It's difficult to imagine life without electricity, isn't it? We were fortunate that our home lights were fueled by carbide instead of the usual kerosene lamps that were used before electricity came to us. Even so, it was a happy day when the carbide tank, which was located in the ground of our side yard near the clotheslines, was emptied and new electric lights were installed, along with a new Frigidaire electric refrigerator. But it was a few more years before Mother would give up her cook stove and coal bucket for a non-kitchen-heating electric stove. Aunt Helen kept both her coal stove and electric stove side-by-side in her kitchen for many years after getting electricity.

Never one to sit back and just rest on his laurels, Dad formed the local Soil Conservation District in 1937, another way to help farmers ("the greater good") while also helping himself. "Always give more than you take" was his motto, another trait passed on to his children.

By the time I was the ripe old age of four, Dad had made yet another career move, this time returning in 1938 to the AAA as a member of the Indiana State Committee, where he shared the responsibility for the statewide administration of the AAA and other Washington-based Department of Agriculture farm programs.

Dad held that position for four years, until 1942, and during that time he developed many lifelong friendships with his coworkers. Because there were occasions where he and Mother socialized as a couple with Dad's colleagues and their wives, those wives also became friends. Not only did Mother's small circle begin to widen, she also felt like more of a participant in Dad's life. Aside from that, however, Mother still was stuck on the farm with four children, a lot of work, and not much opportunity for a social life. It boiled down to the once-a-month meetings of the Ladies Aid (the women's group of Trinity Church) and the Home Demonstration Club (a farm women's organization run by the Extension Service that provided information on cooking, canning, cleaning, and so on), and the Sunday family dinners, which she cooked.

When I was five or six, Mother often would load us children into the family car to take us to watch big brother Jimmie play basketball at Decker High School, which was fourteen miles from our house, for home games and other county high schools for away games. I doubt that we attended all of the matches because, even though Donnie was old enough at age nine or ten to really appreciate the sport, that would have been difficult with children as young as Eddie and I.

It was almost unheard of then for a family to own more than one car, and Mother's nearby neighbor and buddy, Harriet Kirk, was no exception. Her husband, Alvin, needed their car to get to and from work at the Tip-Top Creamery in Vincennes, so Mother would pick Harriet up for their monthly Ladies Aid meetings. Harriet lived only about a quarter-mile down the road, and we could see her house from the big window in our side kitchen door. While my own adventures didn't take me as far as that from home, Donnie loved to roam "the prairie" with his toy rifle, looking for rabbits, but actually looking for a treat from Harriet. A favorite was her sugar-coated buttered bread. Since my only associate was Eddie, I didn't get any of her treats. We had to settle for making our own, raiding Mother's "sugar drawer," one of the big drawers in our kitchen cabinet with metal liners that held both sugar and flour.

Experts who expound on inherited traits versus learned ones would have a field day examining the first four years of my life, the years that would have supposedly the prime time for development of my values, attitudes, and personality traits.

My nurturing/environmental experiences during that time frame included having an ambitious father who, because of his work, was physically present in the home only on weekends, and a mother who thus had to cope with everything and was left seemingly bewildered, insecure, and even fearful at times due to the lack of direct spousal support. My older brother Jimmie had to assume adult duties at a very early age, and the whole situation was compounded by the birth of a new baby, Eddie, when I was eighteen months old, little more than an infant myself. Fortunately, Mother had assistance from a live-in "hired girl," or I don't know how she would have managed everything. Nevertheless, it still wasn't the same as having her husband at home.

I learned several important things at a very young age, and many of them involved discipline. For example, we learned that fathers make the overall decisions for the family and the household, and their rules were to be followed, whether or not they were present. Our behavior didn't really change, even when Dad wasn't there. Mother was not much of a disciplinarian, but she didn't need to be. Dad's message was strong enough that she didn't need to do more than minor scolding.

One of the rules was that children didn't interrupt when their parents or other adults were talking. I knew it was best to keep my mouth shut when the conversation was "out of my league." Also, good manners were important. We sat down together for meals and had a blessing by Dad if he was there, otherwise by Mother, before we picked up our forks to eat. We ate everything that we placed on our plate from the bowls of food that were passed, and we were expected to eat everything that Mother cooked for us. Whining about likes or dislikes wasn't tolerated. We stayed at the table, in our chairs, until the meal was over. We always sat in the same seats; Dad's chair was at the head of the table, unoccupied when he was absent.

I discovered that being the only girl in the family had its special privileges. My father and mother adored their only daughter, who learned at an early age how to be Daddy's special pal. Also, to my brothers' chagrin, I didn't have to work in the farm fields, nor did I have to milk the cows. (Mother, however, always helped with milking in the morning before coming back to the house to start breakfast.)

That's not to say I had no chores. Even small children had responsibilities on a farm, and assigned duties were to be completed in a timely manner and to the satisfaction of the adult who did the assigning.

We had no sense of entitlement, and although we were hardly deprived, we knew not to expect to have many clothes or toys. Again, being a girl had its advantages, because Mother loved sewing dresses for me, and she always made me look fetching in them with my saucy hair bows, anklets, and little-girl shoes. We were expected to take good care of what we had, and being clean and well-groomed was important. Dad especially liked his "girls" (Mother and me) to look pretty when we went to church or anywhere away from home.

My father always shared his ideas, experiences, and enthusiasm with his family, and from that we learned that exposure to new concepts was a good thing. From him we learned that we could accomplish anything we set our minds to.

We learned it was okay to show affection. Father adored his sweetheart "Emmy," and we saw him hugging and kissing her as he was coming and going. This behavior wasn't seen much in "normal" families since husbands rarely if ever went anywhere without their wives.

The most important thing we learned at a young age was that God was always present in our lives. Our parents relied on their faith to sustain them and they reminded us often to put Christ first. They had high standards, and drinking and smoking were not allowed in our home. Neither were swearing or off-color jokes. We were taught the Golden Rule, and we were to live by it as well. That meant that we were expected to display kindness and thoughtfulness toward others at all times, even at home. For example, Dad made sure that we knew better than to track mud into the house because it made extra work for Mother. We assisted family and neighbors in need, we visited or were visited by our Grandparents McCormick at least once a week, and we provided our time and money to support our church.

Dressed for church, Mother's final task before departing was to gather flowers from her jewel-like garden to adorn the sanctuary.

Armed with his trusty toy rifle, Donnie is set to hunt rabbits, but his quarry usually was cookies fresh from near neighbor Harriet Kirk's oven.

Eddie and I were too young to accompany Donnie on his hunting expeditions, but we found plenty of adventure — and fun — in haystacks.

My soul mate, Eddie, and me.

CHAPTER 4

School Opens the Door for the Long Drive Ahead

Kindergarten didn't exist in small rural schools, so when I began my education at Purcell Grade School I went straight into the first grade. Rural school districts were set up by townships. We lived in Johnson Township, which had two public elementary schools, Purcell and Decker, for grades one through eight; one high school; and two parochial grade schools, St. Peter's Lutheran and St. Thomas Catholic. School bus service back then was provided for everyone, even the parochial schools such as the Catholic St. Thomas' and the Lutheran St. Peter's, something that would appall most secular taxpayers these days. The only kids who didn't ride a bus were those who lived in Decker, and they walked.

Purcell (pronounced "purse´ ll") had never had a huge attendance, and it dwindled even more through the years. Eighteen students, seven of which were girls, are pictured in the snapshot I have of the combined first and second grades. Our teacher, Cora Sanders, taught both grades in one room. I made all A's in the first grade, but evidently I became a little bit of a busybody in the second grade because my grade in citizenship went down to a mere B-plus. I remember Mrs. Sanders making me stand in the corner for talking when I was supposed to be quiet.

For the most part, though, I behaved, because I liked school. We didn't have a cafeteria, so we took our lunches in dinner buckets. Mine was a colorful rectangular model instead of the dome-lidded black type. It held a small thermos, and had enough space for a sandwich and cookie, or, if I was lucky, a Twinkie. My sandwiches were usually lunchmeat or cheese; I don't remember peanut butter as a choice. One day I thought I would enjoy some variety, so I traded my sandwich for someone else's fried egg sandwich. Once was enough. During recess, we often played tag, and I enjoyed "catching" Johnny Cardinal the most. He was my first-grade boyfriend. The romance perhaps extended into grade two, and maybe three, but when I met Junior Bateman in fourth grade, Johnny was history.

Our teacher, Mrs. Sanders, was married to a military man she had met when he was stationed at George Field Air Force Base, just across the Wabash River from Vincennes. I think she may have played cupid for another teacher, Edna Marie Deem, who also married a military man, and both couples settled in Vincennes after the war.

My life from ages six through eight was somewhat tumultuous. First, shortly after the Pearl Harbor attack on December 7, 1941, my dad took a new job as the national chief of the Corn and Soybean Division of the Commodity Credit Corporation in Washington, D.C.

Granted, up until then Dad had come home only on the weekends, but now he wouldn't be able to do even that. I don't remember too much about the day Dad boarded the B&O (Baltimore & Ohio) train in Vincennes to go to Washington. What does linger in my memory is my mother crying and how we younger kids were also upset. We weren't old enough to really understand what was happening (I was only seven and Eddie was five), and never before had we seen Mother cry. I even remember the really ugly, brown mohair couch in our front room, where we were sent to sit quietly and behave while the good-bye drama was happening. Poor Jimmie was about seventeen years old, and he would inherit even more responsibilities around the farm. Donnie, at eleven and a half, wasn't affected as much.

Dad shared an apartment in Washington with his cousin, Navy Commander Morris Westfall, who was about the same age as Dad. Morris married a couple of years later, so Dad lived by himself then.

With so many men in the military and the work pool being what it was, Dad ended up being "frozen" in his civilian job for the duration of the war. At least we had the comfort of knowing where he was during those war years, and that he was safe. So many men in our community went away to war and never returned.

I turned eight in the summer of 1942. A few days after my birthday, however, I became very ill with pneumonia. We were lucky that Uncle Doc made house calls or I might not have gotten much in the way of medical care. Vincennes at that time was so crowded with soldiers from the air base that it was difficult to go there, and I was certainly too big for Mother to carry me. Uncle Doc diagnosed my illness as viral pneumonia. Penicillin wasn't available then, but sulfa was, so that's what I was given. My illness created quite a hardship for my mother, as it occurred at the height of her summer work season of harvesting, cooking, and canning. I recall being in the big bed in my parents' room so I would be closer to the kitchen. Mother slept in my bedroom, which was adjacent, and close enough for her to hear me during the night. I was too sick and weak to walk much, so she even had to help me to and from the bathroom.

By August I was finally well on the road to recovery, and throughout that month relatives would stop by to visit. Aunt Edna Bobe, John's mother, brought me a "designer doll" — a forerunner to today's Barbie. My new doll had real hair, arranged in the pompadour style that was so popular in the early forties and covered with a tiny snood, or hair net. Aunt Edna made a bride's dress and other lovely clothes for it — she made it almost worth it to be so sick. (For Christmas that year, I received more clothes for the doll.) Many family members visited me and sent get-well cards. Mother kept a scrapbook with the cards, a list of gifts, and a list of those who sent cards. I have that scrapbook in my memento box to this day.

Before the first week of August was out, however, Mother came down with the same ailment, so Aunt Lilly came to stay with us to take care of everything. What a great cook she was! But poor Mother. As hard as it was dealing first with my being so sick, and then herself, it was all compounded by her husband being so far away. He was able to come home for a short while in late August and visit with his sick "girls."

Long-distance phone calls were rare, but Dad wrote to his family often, and kept in touch with me by mail, showing his concern for my health and well-being. His love and encouragement came in the way of several postcards sent from Washington during those weeks of my illness.

August 5, 1942

I hope you are feeling fine by now and are ready to go to the picnic [at Trinity Church]. You will have to eat some fricassee for me. Tell Mother and everybody hello. — Dad

August 8, 1942

Are you feeling good now? Maybe you will get another shot in the arm. Did you go to Sunday school or were you so pale you were afraid people would think you were a ghost and all leave? Give yourself and Mother a kiss. — Dad

August 16, 1942

I am sure you are being a good girl and helping Lizzie [our hired man's wife] with the dishes and washing and everything while Mother is sick. You better take good care of Mother. She took good care of you when you were sick. Give her a big smacker for me. — Dad

I recovered from the pneumonia, and when school started just after Labor Day, I was strong enough to attend. I entered the third grade with Murneth Sandifer as my teacher. The curriculum was pretty basic: reading, grammar, writing, spelling, geography, arithmetic, and health. I got good grades, including an A in citizenship.

Things at home changed dramatically that fall when Jimmie started college at Purdue University to study agriculture. He pledged Alpha Gamma Rho, an agriculture fraternity, and lived in its house. He didn't have a car, so he didn't come home very much, but he mailed his laundry home every week. Eddie was six years old and attended Purcell Grade School with Donnie and me. That left Mother by herself during the school day, which must have been lonely.

The war years were stressful for everyone as we all had to learn new rules. Everything was rationed, and ration books were issued to every person in the country by the Office of Price Administration (OPA), which was established to control prices and prevent inflation during the war years. The purpose of rationing was to more equally distribute goods, with everyone having the same opportunity to buy food, clothing, or whatever was available for purchase. I still have my book. At the bottom of the front page, in small print, is a warning that anyone found violating rationing regulations would be subject to a fine of ten thousand dollars or imprisonment. (It's a good thing they didn't catch Aunt Edna, who hoarded whatever she could get her hands on.) Because we had our own cattle, we traded our beef stamps to our city relatives for their sugar stamps, to use for our home canning.

Even as young as we were — I was seven-and-a-half when the war was declared — my classmates and I understood the fundamentals of the impact of the war on our lives, and we were happy and proud to pitch in and do what we could. In those days, before the use of synthetic fibers became popular, the silk from milkweed seed pods was used to stuff life vests and flight suits because it was exceptionally buoyant and lightweight. Milkweed grows thick in the country, so we frequently accompanied our teachers to gather the pods from the plants that grew along the road edges. When we played outside during recess or our lunch hour, we would crane our necks to watch squadrons of hundreds of planes fly over on their missions from George Field Air Base, located just across the river from Vincennes. And the front windows of countless homes displayed small flags with red borders and white centers containing a blue star for each serviceman from that home. Sometimes a gold star would be overlaid on a blue one, showing that one of the servicemen had died.

Our news came from radio broadcasts or the newspaper. It was a sad time, even if you didn't have a close relative in the service. My brother Jim attended only one year of college before he was sent home by the draft board to run the family farm. He made his mark in that short year, however, and was elected president of his freshman class and played on the basketball team. Of course, with so many young men away at war, the universities were pretty much shut down anyway, so Jim adapted to the situation and became quite resourceful in both his social life and as a farmer. He was very good looking (six feet tall, blond hair, blue eyes, and a slim physique), personable, and smart, so he pretty much set the standard for his younger brothers and little sister. The family was rightfully proud of Jim not only because of his good grades and achievements in both school and 4-H and his athletic abilities, but also how helpful he was to his parents and family. He was a wonderful example for us to follow.

Meanwhile, Dad remained the head of our household, despite his long absences — often weeks at a time. He continued to send picture postcards to me from his travels around the country. His messages were consistent. He described where he was and what he was seeing or doing. He always would tell me to work hard in school and practice the piano (he insisted that I learn to play the piano, and Mother was my teacher until I got older), and he never failed to remind me to be helpful to my mother. All these were good lessons — work hard and be thoughtful of others — and I believe they are applicable at any age in life.

Washington, D.C., November 16, 1942
You sure do pick out funny cards. They almost make your old bald-headed Pop giggle. Are you practicing your music lessons? Are you going to make me a cake for Thanksgiving? What do you want for Christmas? Are you helping Mother real good? You better, or Santa Claus might forget you. Be a good girl and get all A's in school. — Dad

Washington, D.C., January 16, 1943
I have a big job for you. I want you to give Mother a great big
kiss for me and write and tell me whether she liked it or not. Are
you helping Mother much now? You know you should help all you
can. Are you studying hard in school? If you get all A's the next
time, I will buy you a war bond. Now you will study hard, won't
you? Be a good girl. — Dad

Washington, October 21, 1943
Are you glad to be out of school a few days? Did you get all A's
on your card? I'll bet you are really practicing your piano lessons.
Give Mother a kiss for me. — Dad

Amarillo, Texas, March 6, 1944
How are those music lessons coming? If you were here, you
could wear a cowgirl suit with a leather skirt and a red bandana
handkerchief around your neck and cowgirl boots. — Dad

I recall fourth grade as being fun, but maybe it was too much
fun, because my grades slipped a bit that year, though not too much,
fortunately. Even though my Dad never saw my report cards (only
Mother's signature was on every one, through all twelve grades), she
evidently wrote to him about the cards all of us brought home. I do remember family conversations about our grades.

Dad came home for a visit during the summer of 1944, but my
happiness was dampened soon after that when a sore throat I developed turned out to be strep throat, which then developed into
rheumatic fever. I was in agony. Again, my poor mother was left
alone on the home front, with a little girl who cried constantly from
the terrible pain in her lower extremities. The gasoline rationing pre-
vented much driving, but somehow she got me to Uncle Doc's office.

Without antibiotics, to this day I don't know how he treated my illness, other than bed rest. There were grave concerns about potential damage to my heart, but I finally got better and was able to start to school in September.

I was ten years old then, and of an age when I was really beginning to appreciate having a social life. One of my biggest regrets of my summer illness was that I wasn't able to go to the picnic at Trinity Methodist on the first Thursday evening in August, which was the kick-off of the church picnic season. The community was able to look forward to a month of good eating, with St. Peter's Lutheran having their picnic on the second Thursday of August, the Presbyterian Brick Church on the third Thursday, and St. Thomas Catholic on the third Sunday (an after-mass, all-day affair!). St. Vincent's Catholic wound up the season with the final picnic on Labor Day. These picnics were big fund-raisers for the churches. The church women cooked the food, served cafeteria-style outdoors, and the men set up the long tables on the lawn, covered them with white paper, and set up the folding chairs. They also constructed an ice cream stand and a pop stand, which they manned. The bottles of pop were iced down in big metal tanks and sold for five cents apiece. I remember the Pepsi jingle: "Pepsi Cola hits the spot/twelve full ounces, that's a lot./Twice as much for a nickel, too/Pepsi Cola is the drink for you." Pepsi was one of our favorite kinds of pop.

Every picnic menu included fricassee, a very thick soup cooked outdoors all day in a big cast-iron kettle. It was made a bit differently by each church, but it was always popular. Fried chicken was also available, of course, along with potato salad, sliced tomatoes, and pies and cakes. In addition to pop, iced tea and lemonade were offered. Food service usually began at five in the afternoon, and it was all over by about eight. Regardless of which church they attended, townsfolk came in droves to each picnic and almost everyone would buy an extra gallon of fricassee to take home to eat the next day or freeze for later.

A lot of people think of this dish as "burgoo," but we knew it only as "fricassee." It was a staple at every church picnic in Knox County, cooked outdoors in a big iron cauldron, and was a real crowd-pleaser. Each church had their own closely guarded recipe. This is the one our Methodist church served. As you can see by the quantities of the ingredients, this recipe feeds a large crowd.

Fricassee

2 hens	¾ pound bacon, boiled and ground
1 rooster	3 ½ pounds beans
2 gallons mashed potatoes	8 quarts tomato juice
4 cups onions, boiled and ground	½ teaspoon cloves
1 ½ pounds barley	Speck of red pepper
3 pounds beef, boiled and ground	Salt to taste

Combine all ingredients and cook until no white foam appears and the mixture has a waxy look.

The different church organizations often had games or contest booths at the picnics to raise funds for their own groups. Our Methodist Youth Fellowship group (MYF) had a "fish pond," which wasn't actually a fish pond, but a booth made of a tarpaulin wrapped around a tree. Customers threw fishing lines over the top of the tarp, and workers behind it would attach little prize trinkets to the hooks. Our group had to buy the little trinkets, and we charged only ten cents to "fish," so we didn't make much in the way of profits, but we did have fun. The Catholic picnic events were a little more risqué, since they included gambling stands.

By noon the day after the picnics, all traces of the event had vanished because the men and women would get up at dawn to go back to the church grounds to clean up.

Not only did I miss the Trinity picnic that year, but I also missed the Knox County Fair. That was even worse because 4-H members who received blue ribbons on their projects at their local exhibits got to compete at the Knox County Fair, and my project had merited a blue ribbon at the local exhibit in July; so, it went to the fair without me.

Four-H clubs were very important to rural children for several reasons, one of the chief ones being that it provided social opportunities during the long school recess that lasted from mid-April through Labor Day. (In those days, all hands were needed to work on the farms during the growing season, so school was out in April, rather than after Memorial Day, as it is nowadays. Our breaks during the school year were much fewer and shorter, however.) The clubs were also an excellent learning venue because they were led by the high school faculty: home economics teachers for the girls' homemaker projects and agriculture and horticulture teachers for the boys' livestock and crop-growing projects. Probably most important was that 4-H offered young people a way to learn leadership skills, since each club elected youth officers.

Club membership was open to elementary and high school students. I joined it when I was nine years old, and kept my membership as long as I could, for nine years, until I graduated from high school. In 4-H I learned to be a good seamstress as I moved through increasingly difficult projects, and I learned to cook and bake differently than I learned at home. I also acquired time-management skills, because I had to plan my work so it would be completed in time for the judging competition. I learned to accept both winning and losing gracefully; of course, I never liked losing at anything, so I learned how to evaluate what it took to be a winner.

My beginning projects were sewing (hemming two tea towels, one by hand and the other by machine) and baking. It was in those early baking classes that I learned a way to measure ingredients, using measuring cups and spoons, that was different from my mother's method — handfuls and pinches. (Mother was a good cook, and her method always worked well for her. But the new method was more accurate and consistent, and, as with most youngsters, I always believed that *my* way of measuring was far superior to hers!)

My family became my guinea pigs for my practice projects, and they enjoyed most of the cakes and cookies that resulted. My problem was that Mother had trouble letting me do it all by myself. It was easier for her, and less nerve-racking, to do it for me than to watch me struggle. In time we worked it out, and she backed off and allowed me the chance to sink or swim.

The club provided instruction booklets for each level of sewing, food preparation, food presentation, and so on. In the May 1941 issue of the 4-H Club Baking First Division manual called "Let's Make a Cake," the beginning bakers were instructed on how to make things like simple cakes and muffins, and to report our progress in our record books. We were instructed on how to prepare the work area, directions for measuring, and what was involved in the process of baking (what happens in the oven and why). The manual also included an explanation of why a baker might have success or failure and how to evaluate the quality of the product.

This is what 4-H was all about — learning how to do something correctly, but also learning how to determine your success or failure. My little manual, which I still have, is grimy from batter spills and prints from sticky fingers — exactly what you'd expect from a ten-year-old.

I especially like what the author, Miss Edna Troth (who was beloved by every 4-H'er who knew her), said in the opening paragraphs: "First, of course, you will want to talk with your mother as to when it would suit her for you to make a cake. It is just as important, you know, for you to show consideration to your mother and her plans as it is that you learn to make cakes. In fact, it is more important." Isn't that wonderful advice? I don't recall reading those words until late in my adult life, but somehow I knew that rule anyway. I believe it's called respect for others!

Over the years, as our skills grew, the 4-H baking requirements became increasingly difficult until we were finally making pies, yeast breads, and fancy cakes. I never tried to compete with my mother's angel food cake, though. It just wouldn't have been right!

I enjoyed 4-H. I worked hard and did well, one time even being awarded grand champion (big purple ribbons) for my baking. I still love to bake, more than any other kind of cooking. Thank you, Miss Troth, for your good instructions and guidance that made me believe even then that I could be a winner.

One of the manual's cookie recipes was for a drop cookie called "Hermits." This was a favorite in our family. My mother always made them at Christmastime and only then. Nonetheless, they're great all year. Below is the recipe from my 4-H manual, followed by my mother's old German recipe.

4 - H H e r m i t s

½ cup shortening or butter	½ cup nuts
1 ½ cups brown sugar	½ teaspoon nutmeg
½ cup sour milk (or buttermilk)	½ teaspoon cinnamon
2 eggs	3 cups sifted flour
1 teaspoon baking soda	Grated rind of one orange
1 cup raisins	

Preheat oven to 375 degrees. Cream shortening and sugar together thoroughly. Sift flour then measure 3 cups. To it, add baking soda, nutmeg, and cinnamon and sift twice. Beat the eggs thoroughly and add to the sugar mixture. Beat well. Add the flour and milk alternately. Then stir in the raisins and nuts which have been sprinkled with a small amount of flour. Add grated orange rind. Drop from teaspoon onto greased cookie sheet. Bake for 10–12 minutes or until lightly browned. Makes 2 dozen.

Emma's Hermits

2 cups brown sugar	1 teaspoon nutmeg
1 cup butter or lard	1 teaspoon cinnamon
4 eggs, beaten	2 cups raisins
¼ cup sweet milk	1 cup chopped nuts
2 teaspoons baking soda, dissolved in a little warm water	Grated rind of one orange
5 cups sifted flour	

Preheat oven to 375 degrees. Cream butter and sugar. Add beaten eggs, dissolved baking soda, and milk. Stir in the flour, which has been sifted with the nutmeg and cinnamon. Stir in raisins, nuts, and orange rind. Drop by teaspoonfuls onto greased cookie sheet. Bake for 10–12 minutes or until lightly browned and "set."

NOTE: This makes a large batch, as my mother would say. She'd always wait until we were gone to school to make these, then hide them so my brothers wouldn't eat all of them before the holidays. We thought it was great fun to find them and snitch a few without her catching us. When company came to visit during the holidays, Mother would arrange a few cookies on a china plate for our guests to munch on. Everyone loved my mother's hermits.

Mother also made candy for the Christmas holiday season, usually with the assistance of her sister, my aunt Edna Bobe. These are their favorites.

Divinity

3 cups sugar

¾ cup light corn syrup

¾ cup hot water

¼ teaspoon salt

2 egg whites

1 cup chopped nuts

½ cup flaked coconut (optional)

Butter the sides of a heavy 2-quart saucepan and in it, combine the first four ingredients. Cook over medium-high heat, stirring constantly, until the sugar dissolves and the mixture comes to a boil. Cook to a hard ball stage (250 degrees) without stirring. Remove from heat.

While the syrup is cooking, beat the egg whites until soft peaks form. Pour the hot syrup slowly over egg whites, beating constantly with mixer on high speed until soft peaks form and the mixture starts to lose its gloss. Stir in the nuts and coconut. The mixture should hold its shape when dropped by teaspoon onto waxed paper or a buttered surface. Makes about 60 pieces.

Fondant

2 ½ cups sugar   ¼ teaspoon cream of tartar

¾ cup water   Paraffin

Semisweet or bittersweet chocolate

Cook ingredients to soft ball stage (234 degrees). Let stand until cool, then beat with a spoon to a soft, creamy mass. Add almond or other flavoring, if desired. With your hands, roll into small balls and place on waxed paper. Let cool.

Meanwhile, melt the chocolate and add a teaspoon of the paraffin. Pick up each ball on a toothpick and dip into the melted chocolate. Place the chocolate-coated ball on the waxed paper and press either half a pecan or English walnut on top. When the chocolate has set, store the candy in an airtight container.

Pecan Roll

2 cups granulated sugar   Finely chopped pecans

1 cup less 1 tablespoon white corn syrup

1 cup less 1 tablespoon heavy cream

Combine first three ingredients and cook until it registers 240 degrees on a candy thermometer. Let cool some, then beat until airy. When mixture is cool enough to handle, shape into a long roll. Roll in chopped pecans and refrigerate until it's firm enough to slice. Store sliced candy in cool place.

Franklin Roosevelt was still president of the United States in the winter of 1943–1944. He appointed General Dwight D. Eisenhower the supreme commander of the Allied Forces, and the military budget was $100 billion. The Pentagon, the world's largest office building, whose construction began in September 1941, was completed in January 1943 at a cost of about $83 million.

The average life expectancy in 1943 had inched up to 62.9 years, a movie ticket cost thirty-five cents, gas sold for fifteen cents a gallon, and the price of sugar was seventy-five cents for ten pounds. Popular songs reflected the wartime loneliness with titles like "As Time Goes By," "Dearly Beloved," "Don't Get Around Much Anymore," and "Paper Doll," recorded by the Ink Spots, Glenn Miller and his orchestra, and the Mills Brothers, respectively. *Casablanca* was the big movie at the Academy Awards that year, winning three Oscars. Other popular movies included *For Whom the Bell Tolls* and *Frankenstein Meets the Wolf Man*. *Time* magazine's man of the year was Pope Pius XII.

In my little corner of the world, autograph books were a big hit. Mine was a present for my ninth birthday present, and I put my name and address inside the front cover, along with the date July 17, 1943 (a week after my birthday on July 11). The first entry in the book was from my mother:

> *My Dear Lorene,*
> *Only one life, so live it well,*
> *and keep thy candle trimmed and bright.*
> *Eternity, not time, will tell*
> *the radius of that candle's light.*

Well, that was a pretty deep sentiment for a nine-year-old.

Cousin Alice Ann wrote:
> *Dear Lorene,*
> *If I was a little pig and ran into your yard, if you were a dog,*
> *would you bite me very hard?*

From brother Jim:
> *Dear Struts,*
> *Can't think, pen won't write, so I'll just sign my name, just*
> *for spite.*

From my Grandma McCormick:

Dear Lorene,

When things go wrong, as things sometimes do, remember that you have a Grandma that will always be true.

Here's a really hot one:

Dear Lorene,

When you get married and live on the farm, send me a pickle as long as your arm. — Junior Bateman, your lover

And this one was a "killer":

Dear Struts,

May you grow slimmer as the years go by, but stay as sweet as you are now. — Paul Delisle

The fifth grade, 1944–1945, was much like the fourth, and later, the sixth. The classes were so small, all three grades were taught in one room. We were arranged in rows, with the fourth graders on the left, the fifth graders in the center, and the sixth graders on the right, and the same teachers taught all three of those grades. The biggest event of the school year, for me, was that my best friend in my grade, Phyllis Petts, moved away. I guess the reason she was my best friend in my grade was because there were just the two of us girls in that grade to begin with. When she left, I was it. Fortunately, I had friends and cousins in other classes.

The war intruded somewhat more than usual in the summer of 1945. Jim had planted fields of tomatoes as a cash crop, and because field hands were in short supply, he negotiated with George Field Air Base to use German war prisoners to pick the tomatoes. They arrived in an army truck accompanied by armed U.S. military guards. The guards surrounded the fields, their guns at the ready in case someone tried to escape. Mother cooked big meals for the POWs and tried to speak a little German to them. They were supposed to be the enemy, but we couldn't help feeling sorry for them. They really were just lonesome kids far from home, and they were so happy to be able to work on our farm.

Around that time Jim also became engaged to marry Bettye Gramelspacher, a girl from Jasper, Indiana. She was very pretty, and I was in awe of her. I couldn't imagine what it would be like to have a big sister.

The war came to a close that summer and men started coming home from everywhere. My dad came home to stay, too, in 1946. He was forty-four years old, still a young man by today's standards. Don was a teenager, I was about to turn twelve, and Ed was ten. (My brothers had lost their little-boy nicknames by then and became known as Jim, Don, and Ed.) It was sort of a shock for everyone to learn how to have Dad at home all of the time.

Because Ed was two years behind me in school and starting fourth grade in the fall of 1945, he was in my classroom when I started the sixth grade that year. No doubt we probably told tales on each other's school behavior. I thought arithmetic was fun because we held multiplication drills with everyone in the room. The sixth graders did the elevenths and twelfths, while the fourth and fifth graders did the lower numbers.

I was so glad to move on to seventh grade without my brother in my classroom and with a new teacher, Mrs. Flossie Warner, who taught both seventh and eighth grades in the same room. I have a note from her in my autograph book, dated September 18, 1946:

> *Dear Lorene,*
>
> *We are living in a glorious age. We are helping in the great onward movement by singing joyous songs, by thinking new, loving, courageous thoughts, and by believing in God as omnipresent and all powerful.*

That was a lot to digest! Mrs. Warner was rather stout and had white hair that she wore pulled back in a bun. I'm not sure about her personal hygiene; sometimes she didn't smell very good. Nevertheless, she was a stickler for good penmanship, and had us practice often, writing rows and rows of letters until our hands cramped. I worked hard and managed to make a good grade in penmanship and my other subjects, too. As for my cousin John Henry Bobe, I don't know what he got in citizenship that year, but it probably was not an A; he ended up standing in the corner one day when he was caught passing me a note in class.

By the time I entered the eighth grade in 1947, I had shot up to a statuesque five feet, eight inches tall, and was very slim! Up until then, Uncle Doc had been concerned about chubby Lorene and had threatened to put me on a diet, but fortunately, nature intervened and that proved unnecessary.

I was still the only girl in my class, but I didn't care. My love life was improving, though, and I had a new boyfriend, Norman Pahmeier, a freshman at Decker High School. We had met the year before on the playground at Purcell when he changed buses to go to St. Peter's Lutheran School. He was very cute, tall, with blond hair and blue eyes. He was on the freshman basketball team, so I would see him when we went to my brother Don's varsity games. I felt very sophisticated to have an "older man" as my boyfriend.

Sorrow visited our family in June of 1947 when my Grandma McCormick died at the age of eighty-two. She wasn't sick for very long, and I'm not sure what caused her death. She was a lovely lady who, although she was kept under her husband's thumb in many ways, as most women were in those days, still found plenty of opportunities to express her creativity. She was a wonderful cook who always had pies in her pie safe whenever visitors or family stopped by to visit. She also put up cans and cans of meat, potatoes, vegetables, fruits, jams, jellies, cucumber pickles, and always a few jars of watermelon pickles, her secret ingredient in her famous fruitcakes. Grandma McCormick always had geese in her farm yard, and roast goose was served for special occasions.

We loved Grandma and missed her terribly, but my grandpa was devastated. He had never lived alone, and started spending a lot of time at his daughter Midah's house. Aunt Midah and her husband, Clarence Neal, owned the farm just to the west of Grandpa's land, so they were closer to him than we were. Eventually, he moved into their home.

Apple Butter

This was made in the fall at Grandma's house, cooked outdoors in a big caldron over a fire.

Peel and slice a bushel of apples and place in a large pot. Add 5 pounds sugar and cinnamon to taste when almost done. Cook a little longer and test to see if it looks stiff. There should be no water around the sides when you test a spoonful. Makes about 4 gallons.

Sugar Cookies

This was Grandma's favorite cookie.

3 cups flour, approximately	1 egg, lightly beaten
2 teaspoons baking powder	¾ cup lard, softened
¼ teaspoon salt	¾ cup milk
1 cup sugar	3 teaspoons vanilla

Combine the flour, baking powder, and salt in a large mixing bowl. Make a well in the middle and add the sugar, egg, and lard. Stir the vanilla into the milk, then slowly add milk to the dry ingredients. Stir by hand until the mixture forms a ball.

Divide the dough into manageable sections. Roll dough out to 1/4-inch thickness. Sprinkle lightly with sugar and gently roll it in. Cut cookies with a large round cutter and bake on greased cookie sheet at 400 degrees about 10 minutes, or just until light brown.

Grandma's Fruit Cake

Makes 10 pounds

COMBINE IN A LARGE SAUCE PAN:

2 cups brown sugar	1 pound currants
2 cups Karo syrup	2 teaspoons salt
4 cups hot water	3 cups nuts
½ cup lard	3 teaspoons cinnamon
2 pounds raisins	1 teaspoon cloves

BOIL 10 MINUTES. REMOVE FROM HEAT AND LET COOL, THEN ADD:

4 teaspoons baking soda dissolved in 2 tablespoons lukewarm water

5 cups flour

2 packages preserved citron peel

1 pint watermelon pickles

1 pound fruit mix, combined with 1 cup flour

4 eggs

Stir until well-blended. Pour into tube pans that are lined with waxed paper, filling the pans about ⅔ full. Bake at 350 degrees about 2 ½ hours or until set. Cool the cakes in the pans, then turn out on plates, peel off paper and cover with whiskey-soaked cloths. Store in a cool place for at least one month before slicing.

When Dad came home from Washington in 1946, what had seemed like a rather empty home life suddenly became very full. Don was sixteen and had a driver's license. Jim married Bettye on

December 28, 1946, and they moved to a little house just down the gravel road from our home. Dad had built it, assembling it from parts of salvaged wood grain bins he had bought in Petersburg, Indiana, intending it to be a place for hired help to stay. As it turned out, it was many years before hired help lived in it because it became a "starter" house for all of his sons when they married. After so many years with just my rough-and-tumble brothers as my close companions, I loved having Bettye nearby so I could at last learn how to be a real young lady from her. Meanwhile, Jim had decided that farming wasn't for him and went into business with a neighbor by the last name of Thomas. They established a trucking company called M-T Produce, and hauled locally grown produce — melons, apples, peaches, and tomatoes — to larger markets in Indianapolis and beyond.

It would have been easy for Dad to slow down in those postwar years, but that simply was not in his nature. Always active in our community and beyond, he kept busy as a district farm field man for the Federal Crop Insurance Corporation, the president of the Knox County Farm Bureau, and a member of the board of directors of the Indiana Farm Bureau in Indianapolis. (Originally called the Indiana Federation of Farmers, the Farm Bureau was founded in 1919.) He was also a director of the Columbus (Ohio) Livestock Producers Association.

In addition, Dad resumed his interest in farming and began to expand our acreage by leasing farm land in the White River bottoms a few miles from our home. We had hired help — I particularly remember a man called "Snuffy" Smith — who lived in rented houses near the leased land, and, of course, Don by then was of an age to help during the summer. Dad, however, still the quintessential multitasker who was never satisfied with just one project at a time, delegated the farm work to the hired hands and began a new venture, partnering with my uncle Ray Bobe, building large, round metal grain bins on farms in Illinois and Iowa. This opportunity came about because of Dad's contacts in agriculture circles, both state and national. So away he went again, always on the go and traveling throughout the Midwest, although at least he was home on weekends now. Dad and my uncle both made some money doing this for two or three years before Dad moved on to other projects.

Dad was careful with his finances, but he was always generous with his money. He bought lovely things for my mother, and a nice car for us and for my grandpa. The house benefited, too, by getting an extensive remodeling. Old flooring in some rooms was replaced with wall-to-wall carpet, and hardwood flooring was installed in others. Rooms were painted and a big picture window replaced two old side-by-side double-hung windows in the living room. The most dramatic change happened on the outside when the old wood siding was covered over with a product called "Permastone." It looked like limestone but was actually a manmade product. We thought it looked very nice, and it lasted until the house was again remodeled in the 1990s. The first remodeling was completed over a period of several months, and we continued to live in the house while the work was being done.

We thought our "new" house was just wonderful.

My third-grade class picture, taken with the fourth grade, in September 1942. That's me in the front row, third from the left.

Me at age eight.

*With Norman
at Decker
High, 1947 . . .*

and on a sunny afternoon in 1953.

CHAPTER 5

Dad Goes to Washington

Life Makes a Sharp
Right Turn

The postwar years were an exciting time to be a teenager. The year I started high school, 1948, was a year of great change not only for me, but for the country as well. Three years earlier, on April 12, 1945, President Franklin D. Roosevelt died. Vice President Harry S. Truman, who took the place of Commander in Chief, made the wrenching decision to drop the atomic bombs on Japan, thus ending World War II. Peacetime had brought the husbands, sweethearts, and sons home from military duty to resume their old lives or begin new ones. The GI Bill offered the veterans a chance to go to college and buy homes for their young families. Wives were released from their wartime jobs and reinstated as homemakers and helpmates. Although many women had enjoyed their jobs and the freedom that working gave them, most were eager to leave the factories to be back home.

In 1948, median incomes had risen to almost three thousand dollars a year and were increasing steadily as jobs grew and people increasingly demanded more goods and services. Frozen foods were new in the grocery stores and were stored at home in the new Kelvinator refrigerator-freezers or cooked on the Hotpoint electric stoves. Gone for the most part were the wringer washers and their accompanying rinse tubs, and clothes were now washed in streamlined Bendix washers (we had one) or Westinghouse Laundromats. The hottest new item, though, was the small black-and-white television set. More than a million of them were in the marketplace by 1948, and families gathered around their sets on Sunday nights to watch Ed Sullivan hosting *Toast of the Town* on CBS.

My brother Don graduated from Decker High School in the spring of '48 with the largest graduating class ever, a whopping forty-eight students. As I prepared for my freshman year in high school, he was packing up for his freshman year at Purdue University.

My high school freshman class had only about half the students of Don's graduating class. About a third of them were familiar class-mates from Purcell Grade School, while the rest were from the other feeder schools — St. Peter's Lutheran, St. Thomas Catholic, and Decker Elementary — and thus new to me. I loved the idea of having a different teacher for each subject and moving from classroom to classroom throughout the day. My school days were busy with al-gebra, biology, English, and home economics classes. The classes were fifty minutes long, with a half-hour in midday for a hot lunch in the cafeteria, and a period for physical education at the end of the day. When school let out at three o'clock we boarded our buses and were home by about four, just in time for end-of-day chores. For me that meant changing into my "everyday" clothes and heading for the chicken houses to feed the chickens and gather the eggs. I'd bring the basket of eggs to the back porch, weigh them and brush off what-ever soil and other particles clung to them, and place them in the egg crates. Eggs that didn't qualify to be sold at the hatchery were used by the family, given away, or sold to a few regular customers in Vincennes. Mother and I would make our rounds on Saturday, which turned out to be really good educational experience for me, because I learned how to do math in my head by calculating what we were owed for the eggs.

After chores, I'd help Mother prepare supper, and after supper I'd dry the dishes while she washed them. I didn't have much homework because we had study hall for an hour every day and I did my as-signments then. The only evening activity I ever had was a Methodist Youth Fellowship meeting once a month. For those, our Trinity group would meet at the church and ride Cardinal's bus to nearby commu-nities for joint MYF meetings.

Our only organized sport was basketball, and most of the games

were on Friday or Saturday night. Occasionally, I would stay overnight with one of my new Decker High girlfriends; Nancy Williams,
Ruth Ecker, and Mary Brown lived in town, and Donita Seibel lived
on a farm a short distance from Decker. Sometimes they would
visit me. Norman was still my steady boyfriend, so he and I sat
together at the varsity games, after he played in the junior varsity games. I always saved him a seat on the morning school bus.
He had basketball practice after school and wasn't on the afternoon bus. We would sometimes see each other during the school
day, but since he was a year older, we weren't in the same classes. I have to admit that although I remained Norman's girlfriend, I
was beginning to find other boys interesting. I kept a diary in high
school, and besides notes about friends, classes, and boys, one re-
veals that I had eighteen cavities filled during my freshman year
for a grand total of seventy dollars and fifty cents. That candy bar
I ate for lunch every day, which I bought from juniors who were
selling them as a class project, probably didn't help. But, hey, I was
just showing school spirit!

My reputation as a good student had preceded my arrival at
Decker, so my teachers' expectations were high. My nickname had
also followed me to Decker, and I was called Struts by nearly everyone, even some of my teachers. (My dad is the only one who almost
never called me that, probably because he had picked the name
"Lorene" and was fond of it.)

My first nephew, Michael Duane, was born March 18, 1949 — a
big event in our family. We thought baby Mike was just about the
cutest infant in the world, but then we were equally fond of Patrick
Edward, C. James III, and Jane Ann, when they arrived in 1950, 1951,
and 1954, respectively. After the children started coming, Bettye grew
out of her lovely pre-wedding clothes and gave them to me. I was
really the "belle of the ball" at ol' Decker High!

Every Friday after school, I would ride into Vincennes with one
of the teachers who lived there for either a piano or voice lesson.
Mother would drive in to get me afterward, or sometimes I would
ride home with Alice Ann, who also took piano lessons. Occasionally,

Alice Ann and I would get to stay in town long enough for a sundae or soda after our lessons.

Before the end of the school year in April, we would already have had our 4-H organizational meetings. I was elected president all four of my high-school years. Once school was out, we began in earnest our summer 4-H projects of sewing, baking, canning, or whatever category we had selected. In addition to working on those, I still helped Mother with housework, yard care, gardening, or anything else she needed me to do. From early June until late August, we picked and canned fruits and vegetables. It was very boring, and hard work to boot. We put up jar after jar of applesauce, which involved washing and quartering bushels of apples, cooking them in a large pot until they were soft, and ladling them into a twelve- to fourteen-inch cone-shaped aluminum sieve with three "legs" that suspended it over a pan or bowl. We used a long, conical wooden pestle about two inches in diameter that we moved in a circular motion in the sieve to separate the peelings from the cooked apples, forcing the hot sauce through the sieve's holes and into the bowl or pan below. After stirring sugar and cinnamon or nutmeg into the hot mixture, we ladled it into one-quart glass Ball canning jars, put lids and rings on them and placed them, six or eight at a time, into a big pressure cooker with some water. Mother put the big lid on the cooker, tightened the side screws, turned on the heat and monitored the gauge until the pressure reached the correct level. She then would turn off the heat, let the pressure go down, and take the jars out to cool. That was just the applesauce. You can imagine how long it took to put up dozens of quarts of other fruits and vegetables.

The canning process would stop long enough to prepare dinner, the noon meal. Earlier in the day I would already have been to the garden and picked the vegetables, cleaned them at the back porch sink, done the "outside" work for the frying chickens, made a dessert, set the table, peeled potatoes, then fried the chicken and made the gravy. Dinner was always ready and served exactly at noon. I was kept hopping, keeping the glasses filled with ice and tea, refilling the serving bowls, clearing the dishes, and serving dessert. After dinner, the field workers took some time to rest before going back to work and read the funnies or sports pages of the *Vincennes Sun-Commercial*, or whatever else was on their agenda, such as a short nap. Sometimes, if they were behind on their work, they wouldn't take the time to come to the house for dinner. Then Mother and I would load up the food and take it to them at the worksite. The men would stop their work only long enough to eat, then get back on their tractors. The workday for them usually ended at about six in the evening, or later if they were behind.

Farm work started at dawn, so that made for a long day for teen-age boys like my brothers. I didn't have to get up as early as they did since, as they loved to remind me, I was the "The Princess." Mother was up when the men were, but she usually would take a nap after the dinner dishes were done. After her nap, she would do mending, work in her flower garden, or busy herself with some other more pleasant work before starting the late afternoon chores and supper.

There wasn't much time or opportunity for socializing during the summer. Mother's club activities were suspended until school started and she had more time to herself. Even telephone calls were brief. We shared a party line with three other families. Our phone number was 798, Ring 1. The others were the same 798, but Ring 2, 3, or 4. That meant that we didn't grab the phone the moment it started to ring, because the call might not be for us. We waited to see if it rang once, twice, or three or four times. Likewise, anytime we picked up the receiver to make a call, we would listen — briefly! — to see if someone was already on the phone, and if so, we would quietly hang up. If we had an emergency, though, good phone etiquette allowed us to ask them to hang up so we could dial out.

My summer recreation was pretty much limited to Sunday after-noons after dinner when Don, Ed, and I would pile into a car with the Osborne kids (our cousins) and go to Vincennes to the Rainbow Beach swimming pool at Gregg Park. The pool was circular, with a sandy, beach-like perimeter, and a shallow edge going in about four feet or so to a fenced area where the water was deeper for diving from a tower in the center of the pool. The only actual swimming space was from the fence to the tower, probably about ten or twelve feet — at least that's the way I remember it. I never learned to swim, so I never went to the tower. But I hung out a lot at the fence, visiting with friends. We would spend three or four hours at the pool and we girls would go home badly sunburned each week. My brothers had "farm" tans, so they didn't burn as much. (They worked without shirts, so the top of their body was tan, but they wore long pants, so their legs were white.)

The best part about going to Rainbow Beach when I was in high school was being able to see and hang out with some of my chums, both boys and girls. We didn't have many opportunities to be together until the official dating age (usually sixteen) was reached.

Nineteen forty-eight was a milestone year in my life, because not only did I start high school, but I also had my first kiss. The big event was February 15, according to my diary, and happened at a party when we played post office. I don't recall the rules of the game, but I do recall that I kissed four different boys. Wow! This was also the year when I began driving. Farm kids didn't wait until they had a license to drive on country roads.

It was a good year for 4-H, too. In the local exhibit, I placed first in sewing and dress review (how the item I sewed looked on me), second in baking, and third in canning. I did well at the county fair, too.

Besides our Sunday afternoons at Rainbow Beach, another special summer treat was going to 4-H camp for three days at Shakamak State Park, which is about fifty miles from Vincennes. We slept in cabins and ate in a mess hall (a community dining room), and spent our days with scheduled craft and sport activities, singing a lot of camp songs, and swimming in the lake. The really brave kids who were also good swimmers would dive off a very tall tower out in the lake. Not me, of course. I watched from the shore. As I recall, those 4-H camps were a lot more fun when I got older and could flirt with the boys.

The real highlight of that summer was in August when my parents celebrated their silver wedding anniversary. They had a party at home on a Sunday afternoon, complete with punch and a beautiful, tiered cake. Guests brought silver gifts, some of which I inherited and have on display in my cupboard. I imagine Bettye was the instigator of the event. She was good at doing those things. I didn't have a clue in those days about how to plan a party.

Sometimes my girlfriends and I went to the New Moon or Fort Sackville movie theaters in Vincennes. The hits of that year included *Easter Parade* with Fred Astaire, and *It Had to Be You* with Ginger Rogers and Cornel Wilde.

When my sophomore year started, I was glad to be back in school, and by the time the first semester was over and 1949 rolled around I was well in the swing of things, even though my subjects in school were a little more difficult. I was never crazy about math, so geometry was not a favorite, although I did earn a B both semesters. I continued to take English and began studying Latin. My favorite class, however, was taught by Marilyn Nolting, a young woman fresh from Purdue. She had returned to Decker, her high school alma mater, to teach home economics and be the 4-H leader. I idolized her: she was everything I wanted to be.

My grades kept improving, not because I was the smartest student (which I don't believe I was), but because I really worked hard and I liked the feeling of success. My grades were good enough that I was invited to join Beta Club, a national high school honorary society. The best part about Beta Club was going to their convention in Louisville, Kentucky. We had an overnight in a hotel where we shared rooms with several other kids. It was an important part of my maturation process, even though I don't remember one thing that we did at the convention. We didn't do wild things like smoke, drink, or go to the boys' rooms, but we certainly felt very grown up, being in the "big city" on our own.

I was becoming very popular with the boys. My diary lists several boyfriends that year. Chuck Farrell and Jim Lane were from Decker and were in my class of nineteen; and Harlan Hinkle, Clarence Delisle, Bill Updike, and George Deem, who were two years older than I. Then, of course, there was Norman. He tried to secure his position with me by giving me his watch to wear, but he took it back when he learned that Chuck was moving into his territory. Actually, all of it was very innocent, since my Dad wasn't yet allowing me to go on a date alone in a car.

My social life began to expand beyond the boundaries of Decker and Trinity Methodist when I joined Job's Daughters in Vincennes, a teen girls' offshoot of Eastern Star for women and Masonic Lodge for men. It gave me the opportunity to meet some Vincennes girls, some of whom were my sorority sisters later at Purdue, and to increase my social graces, which were very limited at that point. Of course, I continued my 4-H activities, winning either first or second in baking and sewing.

My sophomore year was an interesting one all around. Don was a sophomore at Purdue and sometimes would bring his girlfriend, Gladys, home for the weekend. She and I would share a bed, since we had no guest room, which was probably not too thrilling for her. Ed was in the eighth grade and had the misfortune of getting the mumps, which kept him home from school for about a month. By the time he recovered and was ready to go back to school, though, he had grown so much that he couldn't wear any of his clothes.

In 1949, Jim and Bettye bought a home in Vincennes and moved from the little house near us. Their new house, a modern three-bedroom ranch-style house with an attached garage, was a definite upgrade.

We had our last Christmas at Grandpa McCormick's house that year, a family tradition that began with Mother and Dad's first Christmas and had continued even after Grandma died. The McCormick family — Dad's siblings and their spouses and children — would gather at Grandma and Grandpa's house at midmorning on Christmas Day. The women busied themselves in the kitchen cooking the dinner while the kids played and the men sat in the living room and talked (some smoked cigars). After dinner, we all congregated in the parlor where a little homegrown Christmas tree held the place of honor on a table in the corner. Grandma played Santa, handing out the gifts. We kids each got two gifts, one from our grandparents and the other from whichever cousin had drawn our name at Thanksgiving (also celebrated at Grandma's house). The men would then settle down to play a few hands of euchre. By mid-afternoon everyone would head for home so the chores could get done before dark.

The family gatherings ended after Grandpa's death. From then on, his children celebrated with just their own families in their various homes. Nevertheless, our tradition of going to Trinity Methodist on Christmas Eve continued for many years. We would eat supper at home, dress in our Sunday best (I particularly remember a wine-colored velvet dress that Mother had made for me), and head off for church. Some of the members, mostly children and young people, presented a program. Sometimes I would be a featured soloist, singing "Away in a Manger." Other years I just had a "part" in the program that I would have to memorize.

I remember the little church packed and glowing with a big Christmas tree up front. Under the tree were gifts to be distributed that members had brought for friends and relatives whom they knew would be in attendance. After the service, Santa would arrive and hand out small boxes of Christmas candy to the children. Then we would go home and jump into bed, knowing that Santa would visit our houses later. And he always did.

When he was little, Ed would sleep in my bedroom at Christmastime, so he would be closer to the living room where the Christmas tree was located. I remember getting doll clothes, paper dolls, sheet music (after I began playing the piano), and clothing.

Nineteen forty-nine was a good year to get sheet music with popular songs such as " 'A' You're Adorable," "Cruising Down the River," "A Little Bird Told Me," and "Some Enchanted Evening," among other favorites. I kept all of my sheet music, and to this day have it in my piano bench. My friends enjoyed gathering around the piano for song fests whenever they came to visit. Sometimes we would play "name that tune." I would play a few bars of songs and whoever recognized it would call out the name. The person with the most correct answers would get a prize. So innocent, but such fun!

Any time there was a gathering of friends or family we'd play parlor games. One that we played when we went to what we called "missionary meetings" (actually, just a gathering of kids from the Sunday school class) once a month on Saturday afternoon at Aunt Helen's house was a little messy. We would pack flour tightly into a tea cup, turn it upside-down on a square of waxed paper in the center of their big kitchen table, and carefully lift the cup off. Then we would place a piece of hard candy, such as a lemon drop, on top in the center of the flour. Armed with table knives, we would take turns hacking away at the flour, trying not to disturb the candy. Whoever caused the candy to fall had to pick it up with their mouth. Needless to say, the loser emerged with a white flour face.

The year 1950 was full of highs and lows, some of them extreme. It started out with the birth of Jim and Bettye's second son, Patrick, on January 25. Just a month later, though, on February 24, Grandpa McCormick died. Because of his failing health due to a heart condition, he had been living at Aunt Midah's, and he went peacefully in his sleep. It's sad that he didn't live long enough to witness what was probably my dad's greatest professional achievement, an event that would have made him very proud.

That event happened on May 4, when Dad called us all together to tell us that he had the opportunity to return to Washington, D.C., in a very high position with the Department of Agriculture. He actually had been offered a choice of jobs, but he opted for the position of under secretary for the agriculture department rather than that as head of the Commodity Credit Corporation. He went to Washington for interviews on July 6, and his appointment was announced on July 10 by President Harry Truman and Secretary of Agriculture Charles F. Brannan. That was the day before my sixteenth birthday. What a birthday present!

The Indianapolis News sent a reporter and a photographer to our farm on July 11 (my birthday) to take our family picture and interview my dad. It was a big story for the state of Indiana and an even bigger one for Vincennes. Imagine, my dad, a farm boy from southern Indiana who went to Decker High School, was now the Number Two person in the nation's agriculture department! (In those days of small government, there was only one under secretary and one assistant secretary in the department.)

Our phone rang off the hook with well-wishers offering congratulations and media people clamoring for Dad's comments. If that wasn't enough excitement for the day, my cousin Alice Ann had invited me to her house that evening for a birthday celebration, but when I got there I discovered that she had planned a surprise party for me. About twenty-five or so kids from both my sophomore class and her junior class were there, including Norman. I was thrilled and excited, and we all had a lot of fun. Best of all, Norman brought me home from the party and asked me to go steady. Since I was now sixteen and officially allowed to date, I said yes.

Going steady meant regularly going to the movies on Sunday night (Decker date night) and to Pat's Drive-In restaurant afterward, where Norman would always order a chicken salad and Coke and I would order just a Coke. At the drive-in we stayed in the car to both order and eat. Then Norman would take me home and we'd sit in the car and neck awhile before he walked me to the front door. I would try to slip quietly into my room so Mother wouldn't know how late it was when I came in. Norman would also drive me home after Decker basketball games. We had to take his parents home first, however, since they always attended the games to watch him play center on the team, and they had only one car.

Dad's appointment was confirmed by the Senate, and the summer's busy pace picked up even more when friends and neighbors gave Dad a big surprise farewell party on July 25. The following day, our whole family — Mother, Dad, Jim, Bettye, Don, Gladys, Ed, and me — loaded up two cars and headed to Washington for Dad's swearing-in ceremony on July 28. Dad didn't have an apartment yet, so we all stayed in a hotel. Dad was sworn in by fellow Hoosier and Supreme Court Justice Sherman Minton. He then began his new job, and the rest of us left Washington a day or two after the swearing-in and were back home on July 31. It was such a whirlwind trip, with so much of it in the car that I don't remember much of the Washington part.

Several 4-H projects kept me very busy that summer. A few club members from each county were selected to attend a three-day conference at Purdue in June called 4-H Round-Up, and I was one of those selected. I participated in the demonstration competition with a ten-minute presentation called "It's All Done with Buttons" in which I gave the history of buttons and showed some interesting ways to use them. I placed first in the local contest and second in the county competition. Back home, I scored big at the county fair with first in clothing and food preparation, the sweepstakes (the big purple ribbon!) in baking for my Pineapple Upside-Down Cake, and first alternate in dress revue. I got my first pair of high-heeled pumps to go with my outfit.

I won a top prize in baking at the county fair in mid-August, which enabled me to send my cake to the State Fair. How exciting it was to see my cake displayed in the 4-H Exhibit Hall when our family attended the fair! My dad was a special guest of the fair that day, and it was a big thrill for our family a few days later on August 21 when his boss, Secretary Brannan, came to visit our farm and have dinner with us.

After Dad went to Washington, only Mother, Ed, and I were left at home. Don had married Gladys on June 30, and they had departed Purdue forever and settled down in the little house that Jim and Bettye had vacated earlier in the year. Mother took frequent trips to Washington to visit Dad, and Don and Gladys would come and stay with Ed and me while she was gone. According to my diary, Mother was in Washington quite a bit that fall and winter. Happily, they were always home to spend the Christmas holidays with us.

Ed was now a freshman at Decker and was on the junior varsity basketball team. I was busy with school, dating Norman, Beta Club, MYF, and Job's Daughters. It was quite strange to not have either parent at home. I had to take on a lot of responsibility since Gladys was a city girl from Detroit and didn't know anything about farm work. Despite my schoolwork and many other activities, I still was expected to continue with my assigned home duties: taking care of the chickens seven days a week, working in the yard and garden, and lending a hand with cleaning and cooking. I certainly didn't have much spare time. Even on summer Sunday evenings I would have to leave my Rainbow Beach buddies early and go home to do my chores, and, after Norman and I started our Sunday night outings, get ready for my date.

World War II was just a memory by 1950, but the news that year was frightening when North Korea had invaded South Korea, capturing Seoul on June 25. The U.S. Army called one hundred thousand young men into service, preparing for American participation in the Korean conflict. My brother Don escaped the draft for two reasons: one, he was married, and two, he was responsible for running the family farms.

Despite the looming conflict in Asia, prosperity was on the rise in America. I remember seeing the ads in newspapers and magazines for products such as Crosley, a radio and television manufacturer (CBS had just begun to broadcast in color); Samsonite (a two-suiter piece of luggage cost twenty-five dollars); Willy's Jeeps; Western Electric; and Kraft, who offered a macaroni and cheese dinner that could be ready to serve in an unbelievably fast seven minutes. The hit of the year was the "comeback" car, the Studebaker. It was advertised as low, long, and alluring, and even confirmed homebodies would start thinking up new reasons to go out, just for an excuse to drive it. And driving then was an economical pastime, with gasoline costing only seventeen cents a gallon. New cars themselves sold for about fifteen hundred dollars. We bought a new Chrysler that spring and thought we were really hot stuff.

In Vincennes and the surrounding community, my family was perceived to be well-to-do and "special," and by local standards, I suppose we were. By 1950, Dad was making pretty good money in his grain-bin-building enterprise. But farm equipment was costly, and as we expanded the acreage we farmed, more tractors were needed, as well as trucks, combines, plows, and discs. Farming definitely was no way to get rich, and by then the farms essentially were supporting two families — the one still at home, which included Dad, Mother, Ed, and me, and Don and his new bride, Gladys, just down the road from us.

We were never extravagant, though, and lived well within our means. I made all my own clothes, so I didn't need much spending money. One spring, though, Dad decided that it would be a good experience for me to have a revenue-producing project for the year, so he bought two dozen baby turkeys for me to raise. He built a wire cage to house them until they were big enough to run around the barnyard, and I was to tend them. It turned out to be a good deal for me financially. Dad paid for everything for the birds' upkeep, and I managed to talk others into feeding them (Dad, off in Washington by then, didn't witness that part!). When November came around and it was time to sell them for Thanksgiving, I got the money. I opened my first bank account with the three hundred dollars I made and later purchased a sewing machine with it.

My dad's appointment as under secretary generated a lot of news. Crowed *Farm Bureau Magazine,* "Not since Indiana's Claude R. Wickard was Under Secretary and later Secretary of Agriculture has a real farmer held such a high position in the U.S. Department of Agriculture, one of the largest agencies in the federal government."

Two years later, *The Indianapolis Star* described him as "the Administration's 'Exhibit A' when it comes to having a farmer running the farm program and selling the Federal government's schemes to the farmers." Dad's being named to that post, because of his strong ties to the Farm Bureau, had been rather controversial. Secretary Brannan, in 1949, proposed what became known as the Brannan Plan, which "would have provided federal support for farm income while allowing the prices of perishable agricultural commodities to be determined by market forces." The Farm Bureau was bitterly opposed to this plan.

The selection of my dad for the agriculture under secretary was an attempt to make the situation less antagonistic. "Secretary Brannan went right into the camp of the hostile Farm Bureau for an Under Secretary . . . ," noted *Farm and Ranch – Southern Agriculturalist* in September 1950. "The move fits the strategy of the Truman Administration in its scrap with the national leaders of the Farm Bureau." It was hoped Clarence McCormick's presence would smooth things over, but that remained to be seen. "Brannan, the fighting Mormon from Colorado," *Farm and Ranch* continued, "isn't one to back down on his principles. . . ."

Dad worked long and tirelessly in Washington. He was often called upon to attend Cabinet meetings whenever Secretary Brannan was absent (something that can be done only by direct invitation from the president), and was active in the UN's agricultural program. America's problem, he noted at a testimonial dinner at the Legion home in Vincennes on November 27, 1950, was to determine how to use its surplus foods to feed the ninety percent of the world's people who are hungry.

"We have the task of trying to get along with too much of everything, while the rest of the world has had too little," he remarked. He saw feeding the world's hungry as the only way to avert future warfare. In spite of the inherent cost of such an undertaking, he asked, "What do you want to do? Spend your money or spend your boys?"

Always a clear thinker who was never afraid to speak his mind, my dad supported the Truman administration wholeheartedly, even when it meant going against the Farm Bureau and other such organizations. He traveled the country giving speeches detailing and supporting the Truman administration's farm policies. In one such speech given in Kokomo, Indiana, in May 1952, he stated his belief that the agriculture department truly had the best interests of farmers at heart, and that resistance to the administration's programs by farm organization leaders was a betrayal of those they claimed to support. He accused the American Farm Bureau Federation's officers of having "sold out for a mess of pottage and Republican political power." *The Indianapolis Star* printed an editorial mildly castigating him for his words, remarking that "Mr. McCormick, of course, was speaking politically as a member of a political administration in an election year."

The election year took an unexpected and disappointing turn for Dad when President Truman announced early in February 1952 that he would not run for re-election. He wrote of his feelings to the president:

> *My Dear Mr. President:*
>
> *Needless to say I was shocked and disappointed when I heard you announce last night that you would not be a candidate this year. Your political judgment has proven very good in the past and I am sure you did what you considered best for the Democratic party. . . .*
>
> *I want you to know that it is and has been an honor and a privilege to work with you for the benefit of Agriculture and the people. I have been doing all I could in recent weeks to enlighten the farmer about the problems of Agriculture in such a manner that he cannot help but vote Democratic this fall. I assure you I will continue to do this and aggressively support the Democrat candidate, whoever he may be.*
>
> *Sincerely yours,*
> *Clarence J. McCormick*
> *Your Under Secretary of Agriculture*

Dad spent much of the fall stumping for the Democratic candidate, Adlai E. Stevenson, but Stevenson lost to World War II hero General Dwight D. Eisenhower, the Republican candidate. Thus, it was time for my dad to come back home to Indiana.

Our newly renovated house got a further update in 1951 when we got our first TV. I'm sure Dad and Mother must also have had one in their apartment in Washington, as well.

I was anticipating going to my first prom in early April, and I was as excited about attending as a sixteen-year-old girl could be. My dress, made by family friend and outstanding seamstress Barbara DeBoer, was a raspberry net-over-taffeta creation of my own design. Norman gave me a wrist corsage, then after the obligatory pre-prom photos were taken, off we went to the Vincennes Country Club. It was a magical evening, even though I don't recall the music. It was also bittersweet, because Norman would be graduating in the spring and had a full-ride basketball scholarship to Rice University, which would take him off to Houston, Texas, that fall.

Dad was invited to be the commencement speaker for Decker's graduation that spring, which was really neat. He was an excellent speaker and delivered a truly inspirational message. As soon as all of the commencement festivities were over, the junior and senior classes boarded a charter bus for a trip to Washington. Everyone stayed in a hotel, except my cousins, Ann and John, and me. We stayed with Dad in his apartment. He gave the kids the grand tour of his big office, which really impressed the group, including me, as it was my first time to see where he worked. He also took us around to some of the other buildings in the area, and even went sightseeing with us at night.

Upon arriving back home, it was time to really get busy with my 4-H projects. Dad was going to represent the U.S. at the Food and Agriculture Organization (FAO) in Rome, and Mother was going with him; it would be their first trip abroad together. They were gone from May 25 through June 23, 1951, and while there, they had an audience with the Pope. It was a thrilling trip for them. They always bought gifts for everyone whenever they traveled, and from this trip, I got a new watch.

While my parents were in Europe, I went back to Washington again — flying this time — with my cousin Mary Marchino, where I was to be the official hostess of the National 4-H Club Camp, an honor my dad had arranged for me. Cousin Mary wasn't a participant but went along to keep me company. The event was quite an experience. Two girls and two boys were selected as delegates from each state, based on their outstanding work in 4-H. As it turned out, all of the Indiana delegates were planning to go to Purdue in the fall. Later, when I was attending Purdue, one of the girls was my sorority sister and the other was outstanding in Purdue activities. One of the two guys was my next-door neighbor much later in my life, a lesson in how small the world can be.

Mary and I stayed in Dad's apartment and managed to get around the city on our own. We even attended a reception at the White House Rose Garden with President Truman. It was very warm that day and Mary fainted, and the White House doctor was summoned to attend her. She survived unscathed, of course, except for the embarrassment. After all, she was only sixteen years old!

We returned home to the routine of the farm. I still had a lot of 4-H work going on, plus a lot of extra responsibility because of Mother's absence. My hard work in 4-H paid off again when I became the only one from my county to attend State Fair Home Economics Girls School, which began August 28 and lasted through the fair. It was a real honor and a fantastic opportunity, and I was thrilled. Ninety-two of us attending the school lived in a dorm on the fairgrounds. We went to special classes for part of each day, and went en masse to all of the special fair events, clothed in special white outfits provided for us. I did well enough that when the school was over, I was one of twelve "Honor Girls" selected to return th next year.

I didn't have any down time to speak of when I got home, because school started right afterward. Norman left for Texas on September 15, and I was devastated. I managed to survive, though, with the help of a few dates with some other guys. That autumn of my senior year at Decker was a busy time with classes in bookkeeping, U.S. government, and home ec. I also took advanced math and kept my vocal chords limber in chorus class. I continued to work hard and was rewarded with really good grades for my efforts, making me first in my class of nineteen. I was busy with extracurricular activities that year, including being editor of the yearbook and the school paper, *The Sandy Grit.*

Mother continued her visits to Washington, and spent three weeks there that fall. I did some more traveling of my own in November when I was selected to attend the 4-H Club Congress in Chicago. My group traveled there by train from Vincennes, stayed in a big hotel, and had a grand time.

Our family got bigger when Jim and Bettye's third son was born. The new baby was named Clarence James III, after his grandfather and his father — Clarence James (Dad) and Clarence James Jr. (Jim) — but we always called him "Mac."

Princess Elizabeth of England visited the U.S. in November of 1951. A reception was held for her at the Canadian embassy in Washington, to which many notables in President Truman's administration were invited, my parents included. After that, my mother often liked to joke by saying, "Would you like to kiss the hand that touched the hand of the princess?"

Some of our favorite songs that year were "Be My Love," "Because of You," "Come On-a My House" (a sultry Rosemary Clooney hit), "It Is No Secret," Johnny Ray's "Cry," and Nat King Cole's "Too Young."

Dad had always kept up a correspondence with me, usually by postcard, but he began writing letters to me that fall. Many of the things he wrote I found to be very inspirational, and I always enjoyed his description of events, especially his meetings and dinners with the president. From the fall of 1951 through early 1953, I felt like I had a real "insider" view of the political goings-on in the nation's capital.

From New York City
Monday, October 29, 1951

Dear Lorene,

. . . I have been on two TV shows and two radio shows today, so I am about wore down. Not so much for the work as from the waiting around and looking nice, that's quite a job for an old farmer, you know.

. . . I hope you get along alright with everything, and I am sure you will. Remember, your Dad has lots of confidence in you. . . .

Lots of love, Dad

In the fall of 1951, my "little" brother, Ed, at six feet, four inches, was the star of Decker's basketball team, so I continued to go to all the games, although it just wasn't the same without Norman. The season began in late October and usually ended for us when we lost at the sectional tournament in February. Vincennes often came out the winner, as that school was so much bigger and had more "talent." Nevertheless, we loved going to the sectional at the Vincennes Coliseum on Friday night, Saturday afternoon, and Saturday night for the final game. We got to stay in town between the afternoon and evening games, which we thought was almost racy.

In early December, Dad wrote to me while he was on a trip to San Francisco.

Monday evening, December 10, 1951

Dear Lorene,

We got in here late last night, 2 a.m. Washington time, which was 11:00 p.m. San Francisco time. I have been busy meeting the press, the olive growers, and some political people this morning and had lunch at Joe DiMaggio's restaurant — the famous baseball player — at what is called Fisherman's Wharf. . . . My big talk is tomorrow morning, 10 a.m. A luncheon at 12:00 and speak, and a dinner meeting and speak again. Do you reckon I will be about talked out? . . .

Bye sweetheart, Pops

My romance with Norman, which we kept going with correspondence, got an extra boost when he came home for Christmas vacation.

In January 1952, brother Don's first son was born. Dexter was a darling little redhead (both Don and my dad had red hair in their youth). Mother was back in Washington in February for a while. She was having such a good time. The Trumans had moved to Blair House while the White House was being remodeled and Mother was invited to a luncheon there with Bess Truman. It was a small gathering for the wives of the secretaries and under secretaries. She and Bess seemed to hit it off. They were both folksy and had good common sense.

Dad's letter to me describing a meal he attended with the president was so vividly written I almost felt like I was there myself.

Wednesday, February 13, 1952

Dear Lorene,

It is a pretty day here again, except cooler this evening and windy.

The President was at lunch with 42 of us in the Dept. of Agriculture. I sat next to him on the right, the Sec. on his left. I had a very nice visit with him. He talked about lots of things, even including politics. We had chicken, boiled small potatoes, green beans, mushroom sauce, a good mixed salad, a fruit cup cocktail and frozen dessert. The dessert was a little higher and not quite as big around as an angel food cake, sliced like a cake. Ice cream with nuts in it in the center and red raspberry on the top and outside. When the Pres started to cut his chicken his knife slipped and one of his potatoes jumped off his plate. He

said, "Goodness sakes, if I was in polite society I would be embar-
rassed," and "getting the tablecloth all mussed up."

. . . During the meal I told him Mrs. McCormick was invited
to the Blair House for lunch with Mrs. Truman. He said, yes, she
was having all the under sec wives. . . .

I had a very friendly visit with the Pres and enjoyed it very
much. I will never forget it. . . . He was trying to quote Shakespeare
about when you destroy a person's good name it does the person
no good that is doing it but ruins for life the person that is being
injured. Then he said no one has ever been able to improve on
the way things were said in Shakespeare and the Bible. . . .

Of course, the police and FBI were everywhere. He was pre-
ceded by a motorcycle, two police cars, then the Pres car, then the
open-top secret service car and then another squad car. Both of
the cars following him had men on the ground and around the
Pres car before the Pres car had hardly stopped. It seems like the
plain-clothes men all had their right hands in their pockets. I sup-
pose they had their guns in their hands. I believe that would be a
poor place to start anything. . . .

Be seeing you soon.
Love, Dad

Going to the prom my senior year wasn't quite as exciting as it
had been the year before. I made my own dress — I have no recol-
lection what it looked like — and was escorted by Chris Ellerman, a
boy in my class. He was nice, but he wasn't my Norman.

On the other hand, commencement was exciting for me, because I was giving the valedictorian speech. My dad had delayed a
trip to South America so he could be there. My parents gave me a
set of Samsonite luggage and a typewriter for graduation. The seniors went on a trip to Chicago after graduation, but I don't really
remember anything about it, so it must not have been too big of a
deal for me.

Norman was home from college for the summer, and I was busy as usual with my 4-H projects. One of my projects was in home improvement, so I fixed up my bedroom, then showed samples and photos of what I had done.

I had been accepted at Purdue University and knew I would live my freshman year in Shealy Hall. Freshman girls didn't pledge a sorority until the second semester and they didn't live in the sorority houses until their sophomore year. Before heading off to college, I did my Honor Girl stint at the State Fair. Dad was a guest at the fair again, so I got to spend a little time with him. He was never one to believe that anyone should rest on his or her laurels, and he gave me a lot of advice about working hard and using the Honor Girl experience to become a better person. My dad was such a wonderful influence in my life. He never failed to encourage me, to offer his counsel as needed, and to reassure me that he would always be there for me.

The summer of 1952 was one of mixed emotions, because there were so many things that I loved that I would never do again. My 4-H activities were ending after nine years of participation; high school days were over; and my role in my mother's life would become daughter *in absentia*. I threw myself into my activities with gusto, though, and I enjoyed every minute while bringing those things to a close. I spent a lot of time with Norman, of course, and we thought we were madly in love.

I felt very grown-up as I made decisions about housing for college, my wardrobe, and what I needed for my room. Selecting the college had been the easiest part of the process. I never considered going anywhere but Purdue. Both of my older brothers had gone there, Jim for one year and Don for two, so it was already familiar to me. In addition to the family connection, my idol and role model, Marilyn Nolting, my high school home ec teacher, had graduated from Purdue, and I wanted to be just like her because she had been a star in college.

As mothers often are, mine was somewhat reluctant to let go, and she had hinted about the possibility of my going two years at

Vincennes University (and still live at home), then transferring to Purdue for the last two years. Nope, not me! I nixed that immediately *because* it meant that I would be at home. I was ready to head out into the world on my own.

My dad and I were pretty like-minded in many things, and I believe the commencement speech he gave at Decker High in 1951 and the valedictorian speech I gave the following year at my own graduation, both excerpted here, illustrate that.

In May 1951, Dad's speech focused on how young people should never waste their talents, beginning with Matthew 25 and the story of a man who gave his servants money, called talents, to use as they saw fit. Two servants worked with their talents and doubled them, but one servant buried his and had nothing to show for it.

I'm sure you remember the servant who did nothing with his talent was called wicked and slothful and was cast into outer darkness. . . . I think we can assume that the lesson refers to something far more important than money. It undoubtedly refers to our personal qualities. As so many passages in the Bible do, this one is telling us how to live the good life. We must make the most of our talents.

We are not all equally talented, but that does not make one of us less important than another. If you have a talent for leadership, you have the responsibility to use it well. If you use it poorly, it would have been better for you and for others if you had never had it. . . .

Some people go through life without realizing they had talents that could have served themselves and other people. Others find unsuspected talents late in life. . . .

It isn't just what you know that counts — it's what you do with what you know — it's what you are that counts. . . .

One of the best pieces of advice I ever heard was this: "Work as if everything depended on you, and pray as if everything de-pended on God."

My own speech, I believe, was not so much a reflection of Dad's speech, but a reflection of the values he instilled in me.

To reap a golden harvest, or to see any worthwhile project through to completion, requires a lot of hard work, sacrifice, and effort on the part of the farmer or craftsman. We would like to tax your imagination just a little, and let us, the graduates, assume the role of the golden harvest, and you, our parents and friends, the role of the farmer or craftsman. We realize that you have made untold sacrifices, and probably many times were near abandoning the project or plowing under the crop. However, to-night, with the project completed, or the golden grain safely in storage, we hope and trust you are proud that you stayed till the finish. This is just our own little way of saying, "Thanks a million, from the bottom of our hearts."

I would like to close my remarks with a few words from the pen of Ralph Waldo Emerson, which I think best sum up what I have been trying to say:

> *So nigh is grandeur to our dust,*
> *So near is God to man,*
> *When duty whispers low, "Thou must,"*
> *The youth replies, "I can."*

Dad was sworn in as Under Secretary of Agriculture as his boss, Charles Brannan, looked on.

Dad and Secretary Brannan in conference.

Mother, Dad, and I were present for President Truman's departure from Washington, D.C., back home to Independence, Missouri, in 1953. Here he is on the train, flanked by wife Bess (left) and daughter Margaret.

I wore the traditional pearls for my high school senior portrait, and the traditional tasseled cap and gown for graduation day.

II
THE ACCIDENTAL PIONEER

Previous page —

Mother had lots of hugs and kisses for me when I graduated from Purdue.

In my college senior portrait, I clearly had my eyes fixed on the drive ahead.

CHAPTER 6

College

A Few Miles on the Long Drive Ahead

When I applied for my dormitory housing at Purdue University in West Lafayette, Indiana, I didn't specify a choice of roommate, preferring to take "potluck." It was a way to meet someone new. My roommate was Jo Ann Kennedy, from North Liberty, Indiana, where her dad was the high school principal. She was a petite redhead who was excited about the possibility of being a "flag girl" for the Purdue Marching Band. She was also a baton twirler. I knew nothing about that since we didn't have a band at Decker High. Our room was on the third floor of Shealy Hall (there were no elevators!), and had two small closets, twin beds, and two desks with chairs. It wasn't very large. Jo Ann was, shall we say, somewhat "blasé" about the appearance of our room, and after a week or so of her sloppiness, I drew an imaginary line down the middle of the room. She could be messy only on her side. It worked for both of us.

In 1952, college students didn't take all the equipment with them that they do now. My clothes, little radio and clock, and toiletries (we didn't have blow dryers or hot rollers either) easily fit into the trunk of the car. I don't recall who drove me to school, but it was someone other than Mother, since she didn't drive that kind of distance.

Our next-door neighbors in Shealy Hall became good friends to both of us. They were from the same high school in South Bend, Indiana, and had chosen to room together. Mary Ann Kenady, the oldest of three girls in her family, was a tall blonde with naturally curly hair, an infectious giggle, and a very outgoing personality. Jo Turner, on the other hand, was short, a little chubby, and had brown hair. An only child, she was quiet and somewhat withdrawn.

Mary Ann, Jo, and I were in some of the same classes because we were home ec majors. Jo Ann, my roommate, was a science major, who spent every late afternoon at band practice. She was thrilled that she made the cut and was issued her cute little short-skirted uniform.

Freshmen arrived a week before classes began for orientation week. We were greeted by President Hovde in a convocation at Purdue's Music Hall, then went to the armory for class registration and met with a counselor after taking orientation tests for placement. (If you made high scores in a subject, you might not have to take some of the beginning freshman classes.)

Because my high school academics were not at the level of students who had attended college prep classes, I was not in any advanced classes. In fact, my freshman counselor warned me that chemistry probably would be very difficult, based on the low score on my chemistry orientation test. I was required to take two semesters of organic chemistry. Purdue's emphasis on science pervaded every curriculum, no matter what your major was. I explained to the counselor that since I knew nothing about chemistry because it wasn't offered at Decker High School, I couldn't predict how I would do in that subject. I was, however, determined to do well.

My first semester included several classes in the home ec school, along with the standard freshman requirements: English composition, introduction to government, and elementary algebra, plus physical education, which was also required for all freshman and sophomore girls. For phys ed, we could select two activities for each semester (they lasted six weeks) from a list of team or individual sports. We also had to either pass a swimming test or take a swimming class. A syllabus for each sport explained the rules and how to play, and the test we took at the end of the six weeks required memorizing the syllabus. I took fencing and archery, plus body mechanics. My medical history of rheumatic fever disqualified me from taking a team sport.

Dad, in spite of his hectic schedule, always took time to write and tell me about the goings-on in Washington, D.C., and other places he visited. Most important, his letters always offered support, encouragement, and reassurance of his unconditional love for me.

From Washington, D.C.
Wed. night, September 17, 1952

My Darling Daughter,

Now that your exams are all over I am sure you have a lot of time on your hands. But I'll bet it won't be long until your time is all taken up.

I hope your exams turn out satisfactory.

I attended Cabinet Fri. and was at the White House to see the President again Mon. on the President's Management Committee. He, the President, seemed to feel real good and anxious to get started campaigning. He is going on a whistle stop campaign pretty soon.

Gov. Stevenson is to be in Indianapolis on Fri. Sept. 26. I am to speak at a dinner meeting in the Lincoln Hotel in Indianapolis Wed. night the 24th of Sept. . . .

I had a letter from Mother today written Mon. She was a little blue. So as much as I like for you to write to me, if you are short of time you write to her first and I'll understand if you don't have time to write to me.

When you don't know what to do about anything, pray for guidance wherever you are and He will not fail you.

I had three Japanese bankers in my office today. They were awfully small men but interesting. This afternoon I talked to about sixty men from nine different countries. They represented organizations in their country. . . .

Do you know what subjects you are going to take now? I hope you have time to squeeze in a little music if it fits into your schedule.

Keep your chin up now and keep on smiling. Remember, "You're only half dressed until you put on your smile."

Lots of good luck and pluck.

Your old bald-headed Pop

From Washington, D.C.

Tues. Evening, September 23, 1952

Dear Little Mandy Struts, [this is the only time I ever recall his using my nickname]

I had a busy day at the office again today. I had to get some information off to the President's train where he is making whistle stops again. He is to speak at Hungry Horse Dam tomorrow morning. How do you like that for a name?

I also had a little meeting about another trip to Rome. I am asking Mother to go with me . . . I hope to get in some other countries like Greece, Turkey, Jerusalem [sic], Yugoslavia, Austria, Spain and Portugal. Of course I probably will not make all of those countries but I would like to. Want to get in my bag?

I had a visit with Sen. Mike Monroney today. He is chairman of the Dem National Com Speakers Bureau. They are arranging meetings for me in Kan., Iowa, Neb., S.D., Minn., N.D., Ill., Ky., Tenn., Ohio, Ind. And Penn. at present. I think when I get back I will be a real politician. The expenses for this trip will be paid by the Dem. National Committee and not the government. Can you imagine anyone paying to have me come and talk to them. Sure must be silly, don't you think?

For some reason they are leaving Sec. Brannan out of these meetings. . . .

I think you will do a real favor to your cousin John if you will help keep him in school. I am sure he will be thankful later on. And you remember it doesn't make any difference how tough things get, you stick it out. People do not like quitters. Anyone can do that but it takes real manhood and womanhood to overcome obstacles. I am sure Jesus must have felt like quitting many times in his stay on earth. I am sure you will make some mistakes in life, we all do. That is the weakness of humans. But it is real weakness to not pray for strength, to make the same mistakes again and again. You are young and beautiful, you will face many, many problems that you don't know what to do. Always rely on your Mother and Dad. And then pray, for I know if you pray sincerely and trustfully you will get an answer. Mebby not the answer you want but an answer surely. Remember, it is always honorable to be good and everyone will love and respect you for it. I am sure it will take backbone sometimes. . . .

Seems like I am fresh out of news so bye bye baby.

PaPa

P.S. I am going to try to get home Fri night, Sat & Sun. Just so you would be informed. You have never told me how to call you. How do you expect to get a date that way?

From Washington, D.C.
Sat. p.m. September 27, 1952

My Dear Little "Froshie"

Did you enjoy your short visit with your Mama and Papa Tues evening? I am sorry I didn't feel better, I am afraid I was a poor Papa to visit with. I didn't feel a bit good all the time at Indianapolis but do feel a great deal better now, although I would hardly be kissable sweet as I have a fever blister. . . .

Do you find many of your classes very hard? Or are they just a breeze for the Under Secretary's daughter? I don't think you need to worry about not taking physical ed for exercise as long as you get as much walking as you do.

Let's see, what is it you go to school for? Remembering that, don't make eyes at all of those boys that whistle at you. Because you do want a college education and that means studying and keeping healthy to stay in school. Sure, I want you to have a good time but there is such a thing as putting on too much "sugar" . . .

Lots of good luck and good health and a wee bit of love,

Papa

While I was adjusting to college life, Dad was traveling the country stumping for Adlai Stevenson's presidential campaign. It seemed like he was all over the Midwest at once, giving speeches in one state on one day and another state the next. His background as a farmer rather than a politician made him a popular speaker who could relate to the "common man," although, after a while, he jokingly voiced a concern that he was becoming a politician after all.

From Washington, D.C.
Wednesday Evening, October 1, 1952

Dear Lorene,

I don't know as I have much to write but I may have a hard time getting time to write so I will answer your sweet little note. . . .

My plans next week are now jelled. I will be in Minn Mon & Tues., S.D. Wed & Thur, Neb. Fri & Sat, and N.D. Mon & part of the next Tues. W Virginia on Wed. I am not sure yet Thur & Fri but at Rushville, Ind, at the National Corn Picking Contest on Sat. So your Dad is going politicking.

Now don't you worry about making those grades. You just keep on learning all you can and the grades will take care of themselves and I'll bet they won't be bad either. They never were. . . .

Between my two sweethearts I keep pretty busy writing letters. I love both of them, so I guess I'll have to keep writing. I hope I get back to Wash. often enough to pick up clean clothes and my mail. . . .

Keep your chin up. Love, Dad

From Springfield, Illinois
Wed morning, October 22, 1952

Dear Lorene,

Do I think I am somebody. I rode on Gov. Stevenson's train yesterday from Springfield to Decatur and then to Champaign, Ill. I had a nice visit with him. Just he and I in one of the compartments on the train. I could have gone all the way with his train but I had to get off to go to Olney to speak. On the train was the car at the back with the loudspeaker attachments on the rear platform. Also a space in the center where a dining table was set up for 12.

All of the candidates for state office in the State of Ill were on the train. One car was completely turned over to the press and several typewriters were really running while the train was pumping along. We could see the news in the making. . . .

I don't know just when I will get to see you but just keep up the good work. Keep that chin up and that lovely smile turned on.

Love, Pop

The presidential campaign ended with Stevenson's defeat and Dwight D. Eisenhower's victory. Dad's life returned to normal — or as normal as his life could be in those days — as he made preparations for the transitions that would occur after the inauguration in January of 1953. Still, in his letters, it was clear that his primary concern was for his family's well being, and my happiness meant the world to him.

From Washington, D.C.
Friday, December 12, 1952

Dear Little Sweetheart,

You made me very happy by writing me such a very sweet letter so soon after talking to us on the phone. Also, I am happy that you feel like pouring out your heart to me. When you do that I will always be in the best position to help you the most. . . .

Now, will you do something for me? Please? The next time you start worrying or even thinking about yourself, stop it right there. Think of me instead. Think of Mother, one of your brothers, of your handsome boyfriend Norman, or some of your new boyfriends or what you want to do next summer, but please, for me, quit worrying about yourself. Besides, frowning makes wrinkles and it takes so many muscles to frown. You have such a sweet smile and it takes only a few muscles to smile and smiles put the wrinkles in the right place. So when you don't know what to do or say just turn on the sweetest smile you have.

You may not be the smartest girl in Purdue but I am sure you will make your grades and that you are one of the nicest and the very nicest to me. So you keep on doing your best and I'll keep on loving you. . . .

Good night my darling daughter, take good care of yourself. Sleep tight.

Lots of love and kisses, Dad

From Washington, D.C.

Monday evening, December 15, 1952

. . . The new [Agriculture] *Secy Benson was in today. He didn't stay long and seemed more interested in the fact he had a private car to use when he came in than in whether the programs continued or not. He also seemed to be thinking that to the victor belongs the spoils, and that meant all jobs, girls, and all. I don't know whether he ever heard of civil service or not. . . .*

Love, Pop

My first-semester class load — eighteen hours — was a heavy one that required a lot of study. Fortunately, my high school teachers had instilled a good academic work ethic, and, most important, gave me the courage and self-esteem to believe that I could accomplish whatever I set out to do. Clearly, it succeeded, because I worked hard and finished that first semester with really good grades.

I was delighted that my efforts had paid off. My high GPA qualified me to be inducted into Alpha Lambda Delta, a national honorary sorority for freshmen college women. After we were "tapped" we were required to carry to our classes a pledge board (an eight-inch square of plywood) that had the sorority's Greek letters painted on it and blank space on the back for getting the active members' signatures. Carrying was made easier by use of a satin ribbon looped through a corner hole that we could slip over our wrists.

I didn't limit my membership goals just to a sorority, though. I had asked my guidance counselor in our first meeting for a list of all the honoraries available to college women and what their admission requirements were. That list thus became my goal plan, knowing that only high grades and participation in extracurricular activities would be my passport to being invited to join.

My new pals and I had a lot of fun that first semester of our freshman year as we became acquainted with college life, and dorm food (three squares a day, and I ate all of it, plus a study snack — probably why I gained fifteen pounds my freshman year!).

Fall football games, freshman parties, and sorority rush filled my discretionary time. I dated some, but nothing serious, as I continued to maintain my relationship with Norman. I had no qualms about seeing others, as he and I had not asked each other to have an exclusive relationship at that point.

Sorority rush was something else. I knew nothing about the whole process; my mentor, Miss Nolting, hadn't belonged to a sorority and thus hadn't been able to give me any advice in that area. Early in the week we would pick up our bids for parties that would be held at the houses the following weekend. It didn't take long to figure out the top tier from the second or third. If you were asked back three times, you knew you would receive a bid to join. There were only twelve sororities, so a lot of girls weren't invited to join any of them.

Selections were based on whether your mother had been in the sorority, your grades, your appearance and behavior at the parties, and anything else they could learn about your background: family money and position, for instance. Because I had belonged to Job's Daughters in Vincennes while I was in high school, I had become acquainted with some of the Vincennes girls who were attending Purdue and were members of Kappa Alpha Theta. I was rushed by several other houses, too, but I liked the Thetas the best. Mary Ann, Jo, and another girl on our dorm floor, Marilyn Lewis, were also invited to pledge Theta, which began in February of our second semester. My roommate, Jo Ann, pledged Delta Gamma.

While I was busy settling into college life, Mother and Dad went on their second trip to Europe. They were gone over Thanksgiving, so I went to Jo Ann's house for that weekend. It was the first time I hadn't been with my family for a holiday, and it seemed strange. I had been home only a couple of times before my parents left for Europe, because I didn't like to be gone from campus on weekends. There was too much going on there. Mother and Dad were back home for Christmas, so I saw them for a few days before heading off to Houston with Norman's parents. He couldn't come home because of a holiday basketball tournament, so we drove to see him. We were there for only a few days, but it was worth it.

January was really busy as we wound down the first semester. Purdue did not have finals then, but there was always a lot of work to complete. The second semester was tough, partly because of my class load of sixteen credit hours, and partly because I was pledging my sorority. We pledges had to walk across campus to and from the houses, and we had to do "pledge" things like clean up the yard, memorize all of the actives' names, hometowns, and boyfriends. If an active was "pinned," we also had to know the name of her beau's fraternity. There may have been only twelve sororities, but there were more than forty fraternities on campus, so that was a task.

Early that semester I went tobogganing one Sunday night with a guy I had met at a party named George Shunk. It was dark and we couldn't see very well. We went off a cliff and came banging down below. Thankfully, no serious injuries were incurred, but by the time I got back to the dorm, I could barely walk up the three flights of stairs. The next morning, I was in considerable pain, so I managed to creep slowly downstairs and off to the Health Service on campus. They concluded that, despite the extra fifteen pounds of cushioning I had picked up, I had broken my tailbone.

Getting back upstairs was an even bigger challenge than coming down, but I had to do it because the small infirmary for the dorm was on the fourth floor. I spent the next several days there. Fortunately, my friends came to visit, and they explained to my professors why I wasn't in class, so my grades didn't suffer. My tail section continued to be painful for years. It, along with the permanent bump from the baseball bat I got as a child, were reminders that I evidently just wasn't cut out for the rough-and-tough life.

By the time my freshman year came to a close in early June, I was feeling pretty good. Sending me to Purdue had cost my parents just over thirteen hundred dollars, not including spending money, and I felt I had given them and myself our money's worth. Other than gaining weight and breaking my tailbone, it was a great year.

I no longer had 4-H projects to occupy my time, so during that first summer I helped out in Jim's office, sewed, helped Mother, and dated Norman. *And* I lost the fifteen pounds!

When my sophomore year began, I was an official Theta (induction had been held in the spring), so I left dorm life behind and moved into the sorority house. Ours was the only sorority on that side of campus, situated between two fraternities — not a bad location if you were shopping for a guy. I wasn't, because of Norman, and I decided not to date anyone else that school year. I had plenty to fill my time, though, as I was very busy with sorority activities, classes, and work with the YWCA and AWS. I had been invited to join Kappa Delta Pi, an honorary for education majors. (I had chosen education for my home ec major so I could teach like Miss Nolting.)

Adlai Stevenson's defeat the previous November meant that Dad would be returning home in late January. I believe Mother was happy at the prospect of having him back full-time again, after so many years. He was home for Ed's last semester in high school and in time to see him play his last basketball games for Decker.

Dad's last letter to me from Washington expressed cautionary concerns about my future, because after my trip to Houston over the Christmas holidays to see Norman I had come home more in love than ever.

Tuesday evening, January 6, 1953

Dear Lorene,

. . . . About my future son-in-law, I would like to say my choice is your choice as I love you a lot and want you to have happiness beyond anything else for you. . . . Thinking of my love for you and thinking of a lifetime of happiness for you and considering the things that could happen to you in the future, I sincerely hope that you will strive diligently to find a way to postpone the happy event until you have graduated from college. I feel certain you will both be glad you are college graduates after you are married a while. So my best advice to you is to have a good time at school, learn all you can and stay there until you get that pig skin. I sincerely hope you can find a way in cooperation with your sweetie to do that for your old Dad.

I am glad you feel like talking things over with your parents. They have had a lot of experiences. Yes, love experiences just like your own. If we can help you we want to. I think Norman is a fine boy and super fine if [he's willing to wait].

Now, your old Dad has just had an experience today beyond anything that could happen to me, so humble a person as an Indiana farmer . . . I have just returned from the White House where I had dinner with the President. The President had as his guests all of the under secretaries and assistant secy's, 49 in all (46 present).

Your old Dad was all dressed up in a tux, black tie and all. . . . We entered the White House in the beautiful north entrance (Pennsylvania Ave.) [and] went straight through the entrance to the Blue Room where we gathered and visited amongst ourselves until the Pres came in. As we came in each of us was introduced by a Marine, Navy, or Army lieutenant in full dress uniform. . . . The [dinner] table was in a U shape. I was fourth from the left of the Pres. . . . I enjoyed it all and could give you a lot more detail but mebby later. I must catch an 8:00 a.m. plane to N.Y. in the morning and it's midnight now. . . .

Love, Dad

At Christmastime, when I got back home from Houston, the family decided that Mother and Bettye would fly to Washington for the entire inaugural week and Jim would drive out later in the week. Dad suggested that I ask my professors if I could be excused from the final week of the first semester to ride out with Jim to see the inauguration. Every one of my professors thought it was an awesome opportunity, and they even let me complete my work in advance. Thank goodness I had those good grades to back me up.

Being able to see my dad's final tributes in the Department of Agriculture, then seeing the inauguration and parade, was exciting. But the best part was being at the train station to bid the Trumans — Harry, Bess, and Margaret — good-bye. Sharing my corner of the little platform was Secretary of State Dean Acheson. Participating in the finalization of my dad's accomplishments was truly an impressive experience, and I returned to campus with renewed vigor. What an inspiration!

It was a good thing I felt so invigorated, because that second semester was really tough. I was carrying nineteen credit hours, a grueling load, and besides my home ec classes, which became increasingly challenging each semester, I was also was taking organic chemistry lab and organic chemistry lecture, courses that had worried my freshman counselor because of my lack of a chemistry background. With hard work, though, I managed to make good grades in both of them. I worked just as hard in my other classes, and the payoff was a bump up in my GPA.

Even with my sorority membership, that second school year cost my parents only $1,242. I didn't smoke or drink, so my spending was minimal. Also, I never bought extra food or snacks because the food was quite adequate in our house. Sometimes we would sneak down the back stairs and eat dinner leftovers if we had a heavy duty study night.

The day before our spring break, I returned to the house after classes to find the girls all aflutter. My Norman, as gorgeous as ever, had shown up to take me home the next day. My sorority sisters all knew who he was because his picture was always on my desk. I thought I would die from excitement. Norman had a big surprise for me. In the car on the way home, he asked me to marry him and said that he was going to talk to my dad.

Norman was on a full scholarship at Rice, so the plan he presented to Dad and me was that I would quit school, move to Houston, get a job, and support myself and an apartment for us. Because Dad had expressed his feelings about this in his letter the previous January, I wasn't surprised when he said no to that plan, adding that if Norman really loved me, he would want me to graduate from college also. Norman was not happy, and when he returned to school he began to date other girls. After I returned to Purdue following spring break, I didn't hear much from him.

We did see a lot of each other over the summer because he worked for Dad's bin-construction business. Dad rented a house trailer that he moved to various job sites in central Illinois. At those times, living in the trailer with Dad, was brother Ed, cousins John Bobe and Carl Bittner (from Chicago), Norman, and me. I served as cook, bookkeeper for the one hundred or so employees, and general "gofer" for anything else that needed to be done. It was excruciatingly uncomfortable; Norman ignored me as much as he could, under the circumstances. We all were well paid, though, so we suffered through it. Needless to say, no promises were made as we returned to our respective schools.

My junior year was a memorable one. The sorority house was so crowded that some of us, myself included, had to live in the sorority annex. The annex was a couple of blocks away, so we had to walk to the house for lunch and dinner if we wanted to eat. Despite the short distance, it still was good exercise.

During my first week back, I ran into my tobogganing buddy, George Shunk. We had seen each other only casually a couple of times the previous year; I knew that he was engaged to be married, and he knew that I was "unofficially" engaged. But when we saw each other again that first week and discovered that our respective romances had been broken off, George asked me out. Again and again.

My brother Ed had just begun his freshman year at Purdue with a basketball scholarship, and he had a car that he allowed me to use if I would do his laundry. He lived at the Phi Gamma Delta house, across campus from me, so we didn't see each other very much (except when his clothes were dirty).

In the meantime, I had been invited to join Gold Peppers, the junior year activities honorary. It was a big deal. We had to paint a green pepper with gold paint and carry it along with our "pledge" board until our initiation. Fortunately, we didn't have to do it for very long, so our gold peppers didn't get too mushy or smelly. I also kept busy with the junior prom committee, the Greek Week committee, and the other activities that carried over from the two previous years.

My academic load that semester was a lot easier, which was a good thing since I again came down with rheumatic fever in early November and had to go home until after Christmas. I'd had two teeth pulled before school started, and we didn't realize that, after my first bout with rheumatic fever when I was a child, I would need to always take prophylactic penicillin any time I went to the dentist. It was devastating to me to have to leave school, be a semi-invalid, and rely only on my parents for socializing.

My professors were very understanding. Some even mailed my assignments to me so I wouldn't have to take incompletes in everything. I was able to finish all of my classes except child development and nutrition, as they were both lab classes, so I couldn't avoid incompletes in those. Child development involved participation in the Purdue Nursery School; the nutrition class was fondly referred to as "rat lab." Students were paired with a lab partner, and each team had a white rat that we put on a certain diet. We then observed the rat's progressive condition so we would understand the effects of that diet. My poor lab partner had to do the whole semester by herself.

George added a little excitement to my life when he came to see me a couple of times. Otherwise, my days were nothing but rest, trips to the doctor to check my sedimentation rate, and watching television with my parents. I was well enough to return to school for the second semester, but needed special accommodations in the house since the doctor didn't want me going up and down stairs any more than necessary. One of my pledge sisters, Helen Allen, also needed special accommodations due to some surgery she'd had, so we shared the guest room on the second floor. It was lovely, with twin beds and a private bath. Normally, we would have shared a tiny room for dressing and studying, but everyone slept in the dorm on the third floor, which was never heated. We really bundled up at night there.

Roommates in the sorority house were selected for us because those in charge felt the girls all needed to get to know different members and wanted to mix actives with pledges, and so on. Marge Carter, my sophomore year roommate, loved opera and played it constantly in our tiny room. I knew nothing about opera, so I was less than thrilled with the nonstop arias. If I had tough exams coming up, I finally had to resort to going to bed shortly after dinner and getting up around two in the morning, when everyone else was in bed. It may have been somewhat antisocial, but it did provide some quiet time for study.

The second semester of my junior year was very different from the others. I was able to take only a fifteen-hour class load because I was still more or less recuperating from my illness and needed a lot of rest. My subjects included English literature, the U.S. in world affairs, elements of democracy, school lunchroom management, and conservation education (forestry). For lunchroom management, we had to work in the kitchen and dining room of the home ec school's "restaurant." Conservation education was kind of a puzzler; for some weird reason, it was a requirement for home ec education majors. We took trips to the woods, via school buses, where the professor would show us how to identify trees. The only good thing about it was that a lot of athletes also took the class. I have to admit that we all cheated on the test; we devised a way to communicate answers to each other so each of us only had to learn part of the list.

By that time, Norman was out and George was in. He gave me his Alpha Gamma Rho pin in February. It was a big deal to have a little chain connecting one's sorority pin to her beau's fraternity pin. It was also a big deal when his fraternity came to the Theta house to serenade me. The next morning, our pinning was the "whisker" of the Purdue newspaper, *The Exponent*. To this day, I wonder why we got pinned. I can only imagine it was perhaps because we were both on the rebound. George was good looking and paid lots of attention to me. Besides, it seemed like everyone else was getting pinned. No real soul-searching here! I'm sure my dad was not thrilled about my making a commitment then, but at least he knew I would graduate, since I had only one more year to go.

George was one year older than I and would be graduating in June. He was in the ROTC, so he was expected to sign up for two years of service as a second lieutenant in the Army. Fate intervened, however, when he suffered a collapsed lung just before graduation and thus was exempt from service. We evidently took this as an omen to proceed with something foolhardy, such as getting married right away. And we did.

As I look back on that period of time, I can't imagine what we were thinking as we made decisions that would so profoundly impact our futures. Our headlong rush to join our lives forever (we thought) certainly didn't make much sense, now that I consider it through the perspective of hindsight. Because he wasn't going into the service, George wouldn't be going anywhere, and I still had one more year of school. Nevertheless, we plunged into becoming formally engaged in June. My mother's reaction was one of blatant disapproval. She did not speak to me for a while, nor did she show any interest in seeing my engagement ring that George had given me while visiting his parents in northern Indiana. I don't recall how long it took her to thaw, but she eventually came around.

Dad must have had in mind how wrenching it had been when Norman and I parted ways, and apparently decided that he wouldn't interfere again in my romantic life because there was no opposition from him, even though George hadn't approached him to ask for my hand prior to giving me the ring. At least he knew that George would be able to support me, as he had been accepted into the J.C. Penney management training program in Lafayette and would start working the store there soon.

In all of the "wisdom" of our youth, we figured that since George would be getting an apartment in Lafayette anyway, why not go ahead and get married in August so we could live together? Why, why, why indeed, I ask myself now. But considering the standard thinking of the 1950s, it becomes easier to understand: Girls then were not career-oriented. Expectations for young women were to work only until they married, or possibly a bit later, until the children started arriving. We presumed that our lives would be similar to our parents', only better. We would live in nice homes in nice neighborhoods, have nice children, and drive around in nice cars. Our husbands would "bring home the bacon" — a lot of it, we hoped.

I was like most other starry-eyed college girls who loved the excitement of being pinned and pretty much expected the pin to lead to an engagement ring, preferably sometime during the senior year so there could be a big wedding after graduation. I guess you could say we were in love with the idea of being in love, and the prospect of the happily-ever-after that surely would be a part of it.

I don't know the percentage of girls in this category — maybe half — but I loved the idea of being one step ahead of them by getting married before my senior year. It seemed like a wonderful idea at the time, but now I see that it was totally crazy! I was sure that I was in love with George and that we had a lot in common. I hardly knew his family, however, nor did I take time to examine his values. My brief observation and knowledge, for the few months we dated, was that he was smart, personable, energetic (he worked a couple of jobs for spending money), came from a farm, and belonged to the same fraternity that my brother Jim had. George was polite and treated me courteously, and — probably most important to a college girl — he was handsome, with black hair and hazel eyes, and standing at a slender six feet, two inches. He looked very much like movie star Rory Calhoun.

George was the oldest of four children — three boys and a girl — just like my family. His mother worked as secretary to the high school principal at Argos High School, and his dad was a farmer, but wasn't physically able to work much since he had emphysema, contracted from years of heavy smoking. Also, earlier in his adult life, George's father had suffered from tuberculosis. Money was not plentiful in the family. During high school, George had worked for and lived with a childless couple (they eventually adopted some children, but George was treated like their own family). They were very fond of George, and I felt that he had learned a lot of his ideas about wanting to be successful from them. George's own dad was always cynical about anyone who was successful or had much money, and thus wasn't very supportive.

As our wedding plans progressed, I basked in the attention I received as a bride-to-be. I saw Norman once that summer. He must have regretted our parting, because he stopped by our house before reporting for duty with the Marines to ask me to reconsider my decision to marry George. Stubborn and bull-headed, and still smarting from our breakup, I told him that his efforts were for naught and that I wished to continue on my course.

That summer was one of bustle and flurry, since I had only a couple of months to plan the wedding. I had decided to make my wedding dress myself. The gown was a very simple princess style with a sweetheart neckline done in heavy, cream-colored satin with a slight train, long sleeves, and tiny, self-covered buttons down the back. My veil was attached to a pearl tiara, very fifties-style.

For my attendants, I had my college friends, Marilyn Lewis and Mary Ann Kenaday; cousin Mary Marchino; Beverly Shunk, George's sister; and Nancy Gasser, a high school friend. Some of my cousins helped with the reception at the Vincennes Country Club. George's attendants were his brothers, his best friends from college, and my brother Ed. They all came to Vincennes for the weekend, as did George's parents and sister. It was the first time that our parents had met.

The wedding took place at our little country church at two-thirty in the afternoon on Sunday, August 28, 1955, which was also my parents' wedding anniversary. As is typical for August in Indiana, the day was very hot and I just about melted in my heavy gown. I had just turned twenty-one the previous month, and George was twenty-two.

Following the wedding and reception, we departed by car for Indianapolis, where we stayed overnight in a downtown hotel, then continued east for our honeymoon. We went to New York City, and visited the downtown headquarters of J.C. Penney, where we requested and received a visit with the company president, a Mr. Hughes. He was probably amused by the newlyweds from Indiana who stopped to see him on their way to Niagara Falls. On our return, we stopped in West Lafayette so I could see the tiny furnished apartment that George had rented for us. It was located on the first floor of an old apartment building on the corner of a busy intersection, close enough to campus for me to walk to classes, and rented for about seventeen dollars a week. We were settled in by the time school started.

As far as school itself was concerned, things were very similar to my earlier years with a full load of classes (nineteen hours that first semester and sixteen hours the second). I also continued to keep busy with extracurricular activities: I was president of the campus Young Democrats organization; president of the Virginia C. Meredith Club, an organization for home ec students; and a new member of Omicron Nu, a home ec honorary. My subjects were tough: ethics, physics, intro to economics, plus home ec courses and the final removal of the incompletes from my junior year. It was hard work, especially with the extra housewifely burdens of cooking, laundry, and cleaning, but I still did well.

I usually had lunch at the Theta house since it was only a couple of blocks from our apartment. Sometimes we visited one set of parents for the weekend, but George often had to work on Saturday, so there wasn't much time for out-of-town visits. When the basketball season started, however, I got to see my parents more often when they would drive up on Saturday to see Ed play for the Boilermakers.

At the beginning, I was happy. I had my own little love nest, living with a handsome young man who was attentive and fun to be with. A dark cloud appeared not long after the marriage, however, when, to my great surprise, I discovered that George had what I thought was a very cavalier attitude about his financial responsibilities. Fortunately, my parents continued to pay for my college expenses, a commitment they had made to me before the wedding.

My last semester at Purdue was somewhat complicated because I was expected to do six weeks of "practice house," a home management class where six students and our professor lived in a large house near campus. While there, we had to plan, shop for (on a set budget), and prepare meals, as well as clean and do laundry. It was rather strange for me to live there and do all those chores during the week, then go home to my husband and apartment on the weekends and do the same thing. In addition to that and my several other classes, we graduating seniors also had to do student teaching, where we were assigned to home ec teachers in various Indiana high schools for hands-on experience. I was fortunate to be assigned to Jefferson High School in Lafayette, so I could live at home in our apartment while student teaching.

Most thrilling about that last semester was being selected to be in Mortar Board, a national honorary. Only twenty-two senior women at Purdue were chosen, based on scholarship, service, and leadership in extracurricular activities.

I was looking forward to graduation and had applied for graduate school since it was impossible for me to get a teaching job in the Lafayette vicinity. Meanwhile, George and I decided to buy a little National Home from one of his fraternity brothers. (National Homes were prefabricated homes that were popular and very affordable for those days.) It cost around eight thousand dollars and had two bedrooms, a living/dining room, kitchen, and one bath. It also had a detached garage and a fenced backyard. I don't recall where we got the money for the down payment, but either I had some savings in my bank account or my parents gave it to us.

Several momentous things happened that June of 1956. I graduated with honors (the first of my siblings to graduate from college), was accepted into graduate school, and discovered I was pregnant.

That last item ended my plans for graduate school, since I was due in February and wouldn't be able to complete the year. I wasn't really upset about the pregnancy and missing out on school, since that's what was expected of newlywed young women.

Dad was back into the grain-bin-building business again that summer and asked me if I would once more like to be his book-keeper. Instead of living in the trailer, though, this time we stayed in motels, where I had my own room. It was a great way for me to make some money and spend time with my dad, since we always had dinner together. I would see George on weekends, and he used his vacation time that summer to work with us.

The mid-1950s were a prosperous time for our nation. Eisenhower was re-elected president with Richard Nixon again as his vice president. The median income was $4,454 per year, gasoline cost 23 cents a gallon, and ground beef sold for 56 cents a pound (or three pounds for a dollar on special). The Korean War was behind us and Elvis Presley was on his way to becoming King of Rock 'n' Roll.

I was optimistic about the future that George and I would have together and pleased that we were having a baby. Our parents were supportive, we owned a home, and all seemed to be well in our world. My pregnancy was easy, but the doctor was very concerned about potential problems with my heart because of my history of rheumatic fever. I was carefully monitored throughout the nine months and, fortunately, no problems developed then, nor later when I had my second child.

With my not-so-little-anymore brother Ed just before we headed off to Purdue, I as a junior and he as a freshman.

Ain't we sweet! College cuties: some of my gal pals and me (on the left).

135

George and I saw nothing but roses ahead when we posed at a ball at Purdue.

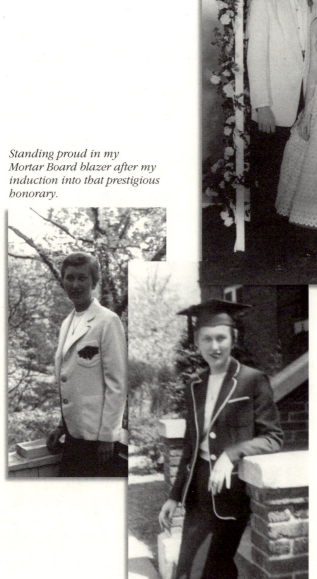

Standing proud in my Mortar Board blazer after my induction into that prestigious honorary.

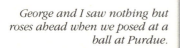

Cap and gown were perhaps not too stylish, but I was thrilled to don the real mortar board on graduation day.

CHAPTER 7

Stops on the Drive

First Job, Second Job, Third, Fourth, and More . . .

After I graduated from Purdue, George and I moved to Cincinnati. There I had my first job as a home economics teacher at a large seventh-through-twelfth-grade school. I did well in that position, and the following year I was hired at a brand-new school to be not only a teacher, but also to equip its new home ec classrooms and laboratories. My son Mark was three at the time, and I was lucky to have a friend from church who sat for him while I worked. I would drop him off in the morning and pick him up around three-thirty, just after his nap. He was around other children he enjoyed playing with, so I wasn't ever stressed about leaving him. Furthermore, I enjoyed the job and its challenges. I stayed there only one year, however, because by the end of that school year I was expecting our second child, and it would have been too difficult to work full-time with two little ones. Baby Stewart arrived in October of 1960.

I don't recall ever thinking about whether I was a different kind of mother than mine had been because of my working outside the home. At the same time, housekeeping wasn't the back-breaking kind of labor that Mother had had on the farm. For example, an automatic electric washer and dryer made it easy to keep clothes clean, and modern kitchen equipment made meal preparation almost a snap.

There is no way to compare the ease of my life to my mother's, and I found myself appreciating her and all she had done for her family more with each passing year.

Even so, I wasn't content to be just a housewife. I'm a firm believer in the adage, "If you don't use it, you lose it." I had worked hard for my education, and knew that by working I would continue learning. Also, as a struggling young family, we needed the money my income would bring. So, as my boys became older, I was ready to begin working again. I was fortunate to be able to find a part-time position teaching a home management class for the University of Cincinnati that I could conduct in my home. Before long, I was hungry for more, so I called the supervisor of home economics for Cincinnati Public Schools to inquire about other part-time work.

My timing was perfect. The Division of Adult Education was getting ready to begin a series of job-training classes for people on welfare. Would I be interested? Of course, I said yes. For one thing, from early childhood I had been taught to help others less fortunate than myself, and this was an opportunity to do that. Furthermore, I also saw it as an opportunity to learn new things and to develop my skills. The job involved developing the curriculum for a four-week series of classes, two hours a day, five days a week, to train low-income women for employment cleaning homes, offices, and hospitals.

The work seemed pretty straightforward; I didn't realize how much of a challenge it would be in actuality. Many of the women could neither read nor write, but it took awhile for me to realize that. They appeared to be listening, but they weren't comprehending the information. I had never really encountered, much less spent time with, people who were so economically and educationally disadvantaged, and I had made the mistake of assuming that their lives were like mine! It was a true reality check as well as a wonderful communication lesson for me.

I had to totally rethink and reorganize my teaching strategy: I had to learn to see things through others' eyes. As a result, I learned how to boil an idea down to its basics, and I successfully taught these classes for two and a half years. What a life-changing experience it was to become acquainted with these women, to share their hardships and heartaches, and to give them the resources to help them find good, meaningful employment, to become more independent and self-sufficient, and thus better their lives. I'm not sure who got the most from those classes, them or me. I do know that I'll always be grateful for having had that opportunity.

⁕

George was offered a new job in Indianapolis, and we moved there in 1965. We rented for a while until we could find a home that suited us. We bought a home whose lot abutted an undeveloped property that was heavily wooded and full of mystery for little boys. Mark was in second grade by then, but Stewart was still my stay-at-home buddy. Often we would sit and look at the woods, and I would tell him made-up stories about four imaginary baby raccoons living there, named Hip, Flip, Skip, and Boo. The little raccoons, much like little boys, were very mischievous.

After we were settled into our new home, I became restless and began to wonder what I would do next. I knew I would always be a teacher at heart, but I also knew I didn't particularly want to teach in a classroom setting, repeating the same lessons and information over and over, year after year. I loved the gathering and organization of information and the teaching parts, but not the repeating. Little did I know what unbelievable blessings and opportunities lay in store for me.

I already knew the value of professional organizations for keeping current in a field and for networking, so I joined a group in Indianapolis called Home Economists in Homemaking. Its members were college graduates who had majored in home economics but who weren't working full-time.

The group's president worked part-time for a public relations firm called Infoplan (a division of the Interpublic Group in New York) that focused on the promotion of products and services. They hired only home economists, one per major market, to handle the promotions and media. A few months after I joined HEIH, the president had to move to another city when her husband was transferred, and she asked me if I'd be interested in replacing her at Infoplan to represent the state of Indiana.

I was stunned. I knew nothing about public relations work. "Never fear," she said, sensing my hesitation. "They provide all of the news releases and tools for the clients."

I mulled it over for a few minutes. I hadn't let the lack of experience with something stand in my way before. Why start now? So I said, "Okay, I'll give it a try."

As it turned out, it was the perfect kind of work for a young mother, because again I was able to work out of my home. In the mid-1960s — that era before computers, faxes, and voicemail — my portable typewriter soon became my best friend, and the telephone a constant companion.

The Infoplan program was well organized and outlined how many hours were allocated for each project and what they expected me to accomplish. It was a marvelous experience and I had a ball; I appeared on radio talk shows, television shows, in department-store promotions, and I went wherever else Infoplan felt I needed to go. I took to it like a duck to water. I was doing what I loved — gathering information and teaching. Furthermore, I was adding to my skills. What could be better?

Infoplan served a wide range of clients who in turn had a wide range of products and services to promote: Owens-Corning Fiberglas made draperies and tablecloths; the National Rifle Association offered training classes on safe storage of guns in the home; Selchow & Righter was celebrating the one-hundredth anniversary of its board game Parcheesi; and General Foods wanted to introduce a new product, Jell-O 1-2-3. Infoplan also represented Brer Rabbit Molasses; Dritz Sewing Products; the International Gold Association; and Capitol Airlines, a charter company that Indiana University hired to fly its football team and cheerleaders to the Rose Bowl game in California. My wonderful photographer, who documented everything I did for Infoplan, got a fabulous shot of the plane at the airport that "landed" on the front page of *The Indianapolis Star*! Needless to say, the client was thrilled.

Two other interesting clients were Koratron, creators of one of the first permanent press processes; and Gevrabon, who produced a geriatric vitamin that was also an appetite stimulant for elderly people.

For Koratron, I flew to San Francisco with other Infoplan reps to become acquainted with the process and learn how to make presentations to home economists at utility companies and in department stores. The company selected two of us to fly to a few major cities for these presentations, and they even supplied outfits for us to wear — permanent press, of course. The trips were short, so they weren't too disruptive to my family, and they paid well. There was an added bonus: The other rep, who was from Boston, and I became good friends, and we have remained in contact ever since.

Gevrabon, on the other hand, was somewhat more of a challenge. They wanted me to do radio and television spots as well as presentations to seniors groups. These assignments involved a lot of homework regarding nutrition and related topics, so this was a time that having that home ec degree really paid off! I decided to conduct a study of geriatric nutritional problems by interviewing nutritionists who specialized in that area and talking with groups of elderly people. From my research, I developed a program outlining difficulties faced by the elderly. Interest was brisk and widespread, and I traveled all over the state to appear on radio and television talk shows to make my presentation. I would end each broadcast by saying, "If your doctor recommends you take a vitamin, here's one that I recommend." Then I would give the Gevrabon plug and offer a coupon toward its purchase, available by calling or writing the station host. The coupon requests also provided good demographic information for my client.

In late 1972, I was on an early morning (6 to 7 a.m.) program on WRTV in Indianapolis called *Today in Indiana*. The host, Harry Martin, was genial, short, and overweight. As we talked about my nutritional program, Harry commented on how he needed to lose weight. In my usual straightforward manner, I agreed with him. We wound up the interview with my standard Gevrabon coupon offer along with my post office box address. I also mentioned that my teenage son, Mark, would be addressing listeners' envelopes, since he was learning to type. The mail poured in, often with notes to Mark, and sometimes a little money, from a quarter to a dollar, was included.

A couple of weeks later, I called Harry and told him about the great response. He was enthusiastic. "Why don't you come back on the show?" he asked. "And this time bring Mark with his typewriter." We did. Then we got more mail. After a while, Harry called me and said, "Why don't you call the red phone on my news desk every Friday morning just before seven and harass me about losing weight?" That turned out to be a popular spot. I'd call in, and Harry would say, "There's that skinny weight-watcher witch on the line." People ate it up.

Meanwhile, I had collaborated with a dietician from the Marion County Extension Service and developed a diet booklet called *The Live Younger Food Plan*. It contained nutritional information, eating plans and food exchanges, plus tasty, low-calorie recipes; the Indianapolis Power and Light Company agreed to underwrite the printing costs. One day, Harry and I were talking off-air and came up with the idea to start a TV diet club. We called it "The Indianapolis Top 500," a take-off on the race name, and it ran for five months in 1973, from the first of January through the end of May. Every Friday morning I'd go on Harry's show and talk about the diet plan. To enroll, people needed only to write and tell us how much they weighed and how much they wanted to lose. (Fortunately, the mail was handled by the Extension Service, which was a boon because we ended up with ten thousand members!) We sent members a copy of *The Live Younger Food Plan*, and they kept in touch and let us know how the plan was working for them.

Behind the scenes, I referred to the program as a "community nutrition project." The dietician was on Harry's show on another day of the week, and she and I enlisted an exercise specialist to be on the show yet another day, which gave us three days of TV coverage to talk about good nutrition, dieting, and exercise. Harry lost thirty pounds, and we began to get reports of others who were losing on the plan, too. It was so popular that six executives at Stark, Wetzel Foods, Inc., joined, calling themselves "the hungry six." As success stories came in, I began inviting some of those people to appear on the show with me on Fridays.

We got a terrific bonus when other corporations endorsed it by encouraging their employees to enroll. Some of the companies even offered terrific prizes for the biggest losers. Truly, everyone who lost was a winner.

Around this time my membership in HEIH once more proved to be a valuable networking resource. A fellow member had heard of a part-time job lead from a neighbor who worked for the Jenn-Air Corporation. Jenn-Air had developed a new grill for in-the-kitchen use and they were looking for a freelance home economist to help promote it. Was I interested? my friend wondered. You bet I was! I followed up on the lead and got the job. Any time Jenn-Air needed a home economist to make presentations at trade shows and home shows, or to be a media spokesperson, I was the one they called. It was good experience in several ways, particularly as I continued to gain presentation and communication skills.

My world at that time didn't revolve just around job and family. I continued my lifelong tradition of keeping as active as possible in as many ways as possible, and during the time I was doing work for pay, I also was doing a lot of work for no pay. I was involved at my church, my children's school, with the Meals on Wheels program, and the Purdue Home Economics Alumni Association, and I served on an Indianapolis Chamber of Commerce Consumer Affairs Committee. Furthermore, I was moving up the ladder as an officer in the Indiana Home Economics Association and also served as president of the Home Economists in Homemaking.

Besides the obvious benefits of being involved in a professional organization, I also see it as a way of giving back to your profession as repayment for what it does for you and what it means in your life.

By the late 1960s, I had become highly visible as "Home Economist Lorene Shunk," and was frequently sought after as a speaker and for appearances on radio and television shows, even beyond my client representations for Infoplan.

My younger brother, Ed, was president of the Indiana State Fair Board in 1969, and he came up against a problem when the director of the Woman's Building (now called the Home and Family Arts Building), because of health problems, was unable to complete her responsibilities for the fair. The displays and programs in that building have always been a key component of the event, and they needed a replacement pronto. Because of my background and experience, Ed suggested me for the position of acting director, and when contacted about it, I accepted. This was in May, and everything about the Woman's Building programs needed to be updated for the ten-day run of the State Fair, which was in late August. To say I was faced with a real challenge would be an understatement.

I wanted to bring more life to the Woman's Building, which up until then had a "museum" atmosphere with a lot of exhibits. The exhibits would be kept, of course, but my committee and I also developed a series of programs designed to make people want to come in. For example, each day would begin with "eye-openers," informal in-the-round sessions (free, but available by ticket only) featuring guest speakers and offering coffee and doughnuts to attendees.

Other presentations and speakers were scheduled throughout each day, and in order to accomplish these we had to redesign the building's interior somewhat. The main floor had been dominated by a huge runway, which traditionally had been used for daily style shows presented by the L.S. Ayres department store. Everyone loved those shows, including me. That year, although Ayres was still participating in the fair, they had decided to discontinue the shows. Because there was now no real purpose for the runway, we had it removed and devised a modular stage that would be made up of movable blocks that could be divided into two or more platforms or into any shape we needed. Our series, which covered a variety of aspects of women's lives, was extremely successful, and the Woman's Building won a blue ribbon that year (along with the Manufacturers Building) for showing the most improvement. I was the acting director for only six months, but it was a major learning experience.

In the time leading up to the fair and during it, I gave newspaper interviews and went on numerous radio and television shows talking about it, and once again, my media exposure resulted in several good things happening for me. One local network TV station offered me a daily spot on their noon news broadcast, and I was also asked to do a daily radio show. Evidently, my work and visibility were good for promoting the science and art of home economics itself. The real icing on the cake that year came when I was notified that I had been nominated for *Forecast* magazine's first "Outstanding Home Economist of the Year" award.

All of these projects and the potential they offered were wonderful opportunities, but I had to consider how they would affect my family and how we would sort them out. For myself, it wasn't too difficult because the bulk of my work was done during the day while the boys were in school. Even so, I negotiated with both the radio and the television stations for more flexibility. The TV station agreed to let me tape my segments, called *Ladies' Touch with Lorene Shunk*. I planned the shows myself, and each three- to five-minute segment covered topics I selected, ranging from how to make three meals from one chicken, to how to plan a spring brunch, to how to make a man's tie. Regarding that last segment, amazingly, more than three hundred people requested the pattern for the tie, which I thought was free. I learned after it was offered that there was in fact a charge. However, the station agreed to pick up the tab because those three hundred requests turned out to be pretty good demographic information they could use for marketing research. I had a lot of fun doing those shows, and I got to work with some interesting people, including David Letterman, who at that time was the weatherman on the noon news for what later became WTHR (Channel 13).

The radio show, which I did for more than a year, consisted of fifteen-minute segments taped on location at local shopping centers. Once more, I was able to tape at my own convenience. I was truly fortunate that I could make my own schedule.

I did win *Forecast* magazine's Outstanding Home Economist

award in 1970, and it was exciting. The awards presentation was held at the American Home Economics Association convention in Cleveland, Ohio. My sons, husband, parents, and I made the trip for the event, where I received a check for one thousand dollars at a wonderful presentation party.

Because of this award, I now was referred to as "nationally recognized home economist Lorene Shunk," and my promotional services became even more sought after.

My plate was pretty full then, but I'd never let anything like that slow me down when an idea for a project took hold of me. I wrote and taped, at my own expense, two hundred one-minute radio spots called *Lifestyles with Lorene*. Because these were my own personal project, I had to really get out and hustle in order to sell them to radio stations. They weren't a big seller, but I at least covered my costs.

Things continued to unfold in my life, and there always seemed to be new challenges. Sometimes I wondered how I could possibly keep up. But I kept faith and prayed for guidance and strength. Surely I was supposed to go down this path, and I believed the events that occurred must be God's plan for me. Only time, and His will, would determine the final outcome. Even so, at times things looked rather dark and frustration occasionally reared its ugly head; but somehow things all fell into place.

Junior High Class Sews Stuffed Animals;
Seamstresses Earn 'Operator Licenses'

The Gargoyle, *Cincinnati's Hughes High School newspaper, featured my seventh-grade home ec class in 1958 when they made stuffed animals for a charity project.*

My guys and me just before we moved to Indianapolis.

Working for Infoplan, I gave demonstrations, promoted a variety of products, and even had the opportunity to present a 100th Anniversary edition of Parcheesi to Indiana Governor Roger Branigan.

148

Before long I was doing guest spots on radio and TV programs, but the best was having my own syndicated television feature, "Saving You Time and Saving You Money." Aired in a three-state market, I offered "how-to-buy" tips and other useful advice

CHAPTER 8

The Scenery Changes, and the Drive Accelerates

By 1972, I had settled into a comfortable routine. My professional life was satisfying and active — about as active as I wanted it at that time.

One day late that year I got a phone call from a woman named Liz Carpenter, in Washington, D.C., who was an associate with a large public relations firm. One of her clients, Miles Laboratories, was in search of a public relations manager. I had been recommended to her by the American Home Economics Association, and she wondered if I would be interested in the job. It would be an on-site position at Miles' headquarters in Elkhart, Indiana, many miles from where I lived.

Of course, I told her I would like to know more about the position, so she set up an interview for me to go to the Elkhart offices. Meanwhile, I did some homework of my own. I contacted some people I knew at the ad agency Ruben, Montgomery Associates in Indianapolis, who had represented the State Fair when I was there, and asked if they had any tips for the interview. They advised me on salary ranges and questions to ask regarding the job — things I wouldn't have known about. I went to the interview at Miles well armed; afterward, I realized the job would be much more demanding than I wanted or could handle at that time, and that uprooting and moving my family would have been very disruptive and difficult for everyone.

But the effort was not wasted. As a result of my consultation, Ruben, Montgomery offered me a full-time job. I really had to think about how I would manage working that much with two sons, one in junior high and one in high school, and how I could keep up with the housework. In addition, I would need to resign from all of my freelance assignments. I talked it over in detail with my family, and in the end they helped me make the decision to accept the job.

This would be a big undertaking, but with the "get-it-done" attitude instilled in me from childhood, I organized ahead of time what would be required to keep things running smoothly at home. From the time the boys were tiny, their father and I had set fairly strict rules for behavior and accountability, including having household chores, so the prospect of their pitching in with extra help met no resistance at all. I made four lists: The first one itemized everything that needed to be done in our household. The second included things I would continue doing in whatever limited spare time I had.

Miscellaneous other chores and whose responsibility they would be comprised the third list. We had a family meeting for the boys and their dad to decide what they would do. For instance, I would plan the meals, do the shopping, and prepare dinner. Someone else could do the clean-up, and load and empty the dishwasher. I made instruction charts for the appliances and taped them for easy reference. The leftover jobs, itemized on list four, would be hired out. The surprise was that when the boys realized they could make spending money by doing some of those chores, they decided they would do them. I explained that they would be expected to do them as well as a hired person. They agreed, and we were off and running.

I was given the title of director of consumer services at Ruben, Montgomery. I was the spokesperson for clients such as American Red Ball Moving Company, for whom I wrote brochures about how to move, and I did its radio spots; and County Line Cheese, for whom I created cheese recipes for brochures, created its television spots, and did TV appearances as its consumer consultant. For Hurst Beans, I created recipes — one was "Beenie Bars," a high-protein brownie-like snack made with mashed pinto beans, chocolate cake mix, chocolate pudding mix, eggs, and milk — and I did promotional work. But the most exciting assignment was writing and taping sixty-five five-minute television spots called *Saving You Time and Saving You Money*. They were sponsored by Ayr-Way department stores (now Target) and ran in their three-state market. The scripts were then made into newspaper columns which ran in neighborhood papers. Some of the TV shows were put on continuous loops to run in the retail stores. For instance, if the chain was having a sale

Changes on the Home Front

As if taking on a new job wasn't enough, my family and I moved into a new house around the same time. The home we moved to was by no means a "standard" house.

I had done some freelance work for the Indianapolis Power and Light Company, and in late 1972 they contacted me about designing a new kind of home for their home show — one that reflected the changing needs of women of the seventies. It was called the "Live Younger" home. I set out to design a house to fit the way a family actually lived. It seemed to me that builders, for the most part, never asked women what they wanted, and furthermore, didn't seem to care.

I designed an open, airy kitchen by the family room, so a woman could prepare a meal without being separated from the rest of the family. An easily accessible laundry area was another important factor. Putting laundry facilities in the basement or garage certainly didn't make a woman feel important about her role as a home manager, I believed, so I located those near the main living area also, one way of taking some of the drudgery out of that chore. A pop-down ironing board was concealed in a shallow cabinet, ready to use for quick touch-ups, and it could be put out of sight with a touch of a finger. (That's a feature I still use in my homes.)

My home was living proof of the radio commercials I did for Power and Light that ended with the motto, "Tomorrow everything will be clean and electric."

on tires, it would run my show on "How to Decide What Kind of Tire to Buy." Those spots were very successful for the company. In the meantime, I also worked with Weight Watchers, who had heard me on my radio diet club.

There's always something new and different going on in an ad agency, and I found the variety stimulating. One innovative project involved my going to a shopping center or parking lot near a client's place of business with my tape recorder to interview people. We conducted some of these for American Fletcher National Bank to find out what frustrated or pleased its customers. Another was for Hook Drug Stores to learn about what their customers liked or disliked. After several months of this information gathering (sometimes a photographer would go with me to take pictures) we made presentations to the clients, using snippets and photos from my interviews. It blew them away! They had not paid for this service — Ruben, Montgomery did — but it resulted in the agency being hired to create major new ad campaigns.

I also continued to give speeches, and to be involved at Purdue and the local, state, and national Home Economics Associations. Somehow I also managed to have a personal life. Believe me, it wasn't easy!

In the summer of 1975, after I'd been at Ruben, Montgomery for about three years, I received a phone call from Louis Jenn of the Jenn-Air Corporation, which made kitchen stoves and ranges with built-in grills and for whom I'd done some freelance work a few years before. He requested a luncheon meeting with me, and I remember saying as I went out the door, "I'm going to see if I can get the Jenn account for the agency." The luncheon took an unexpected turn, because, as it turned out, it was *me* Louis Jenn wanted, as the first director of consumer services for Jenn-Air.

The offer stunned me. What to do, what to do? My older son, Mark, was a senior in high school and was headed for college soon, and my younger son, Stewart, had just started high school. Compounding the problem, my marriage had been deteriorating for some time, and I now was separated from my husband of nineteen years and on the verge of divorce. Furthermore, I loved my job at Ruben, Montgomery.

Sensing my indecision, Louis Jenn sweetened his offer by doubling the salary I was making at the agency, and threw in a company car, to boot. How could I possibly say no to that? I couldn't, so I reluctantly resigned my comfortable and much-enjoyed job at the agency and began my new adventure at Jenn-Air.

I was coming into brand-new territory and big new challenges. Jenn-Air had never had a consumer services director, so my first goal was to establish the guidelines of the job. My new department would manage consumer information and complaints, and would work with the advertising, sales, and marketing managers to promote Jenn-Air products. A new facility was under construction to house the department, and besides lovely new offices, it would also house a demonstration kitchen and small auditorium. The new quarters were open a few months after I started there, and we were up and running!

The Jenn-Air grills were remarkable and revolutionary. They were designed for indoor use, which made grilling a year-round possibility, essentially unheard of in those days. The secret to the success of the indoor grill was its patented downdraft ventilation built in and vented to the outside. A substantial part of my new job was to visit major cities in the continental U.S. where there was a strong Jenn-Air distributor, and make presentations on the best way to sell the grills and full-sized ranges with interchangeable cooktops also featuring downdraft ventilation. Here I was, a farm girl who had never really roamed far from home — and certainly never alone. Now I was doing a lot of traveling, each trip averaging three days and two nights. I really had to know my stuff, too, because I was operating in a man's world, with two presentations, one each evening, to builders and Jenn-Air dealers. These presentations usually were held in a hotel ballroom, unless a distributor had a large enough showroom for the event, and involved a cocktail party and dinner. Following that would be my program, where I demonstrated the best selling techniques. You could say our motto was, "Let them eat steak." Never talk hot dogs or hamburgers, because, of course, anyone who bought a Jenn-Air believed he would always eat steak!

Jenn-Air Corporation was on the cutting edge of the development of many innovative new products, and I was proud to be a part of that process. When I joined the company, the research department was finalizing the design of the first convection oven intended for general consumer use. There were a lot of commercial convection ovens in restaurants, especially in Europe, but none yet manufactured for homes. I was assigned to research the concept, test the various uses of the oven for homemakers, and develop a use-and-care manual to go with the product. Thank goodness for the wonderful science-based curriculum at Purdue and the physics I'd had to take in order to graduate! In researching the convection oven I learned more about air flow and heat conduction than I ever thought was possible. For example, our research showed that three sheets of cookies could be baked simultaneously because of the circulating heated air, so we recommended that the ovens be sold with three racks instead of two. All convection ovens are now sold that way. Other materials I developed while there also became the standard for the industry.

In 1978, the last year I was with Jenn-Air, Louis Jenn decided to take the company public, an exciting experience. I was given a generous stock package as a thank-you for my contributions to the company's success.

⁂

After three years of wonderful work opportunities, I was feeling the urge to conquer new territory. Once again an offer came along that was too good to refuse. During my time at Ruben, Montgomery, I met Marvin Herb, who at that time had been president of Indianapolis Pepsi (then owned by Borden, Inc.), when Pepsi had been an agency client. Borden had several divisions — Food, Dairy, International, Institutional, and so on — and Marvin had been promoted to president of the Dairy Division. He called one day in August of 1978 and asked to meet with me in Columbus, Ohio, where the Borden corporate offices were located. I agree to stop there on my way back from a trip to Virginia.

To my surprise, he offered me the opportunity to be the first director of new product development of Borden's Dairy Division. Marvin was planning to move the executives of the Dairy Division to Houston, Texas, including me, if I accepted the position. I couldn't believe my ears! What did *I* know about product development? But, as in college when faced with having to take chemistry — and succeeding — I knew I could and would learn if I worked at it hard enough. Besides, if there was one thing I did know about from growing up on a farm, it was cows and dairies! I accepted.

I had roughly two months to pull things together before I headed to Houston in October. Fortunately, I didn't have to worry about disrupting my sons' lives. Both boys were in college by then, Mark a senior and Stewart a freshman, and more or less on their own, anyway. There was a house to sell in Indy, however, a car to purchase (no more company car), and a house to buy in Houston, a city I had visited several times but about which I knew very little. I knew only one person in Houston, a home economist who worked for the Jenn-Air distributor there. Moving so far away by myself was definitely a stretch by anyone's definition, and a daunting prospect.

Once more I had to put on my serious creative hat; just as with my position at Jenn-Air, the responsibilities of my new job needed to be defined and I had to build it from the ground up. I would be working in conjunction with the Borden Research Department in Syracuse, New York, as well as the home economists, legal staff, and plant operations personnel back in Columbus, Ohio.

My job included locating, acquiring, or creating new product concepts, processes, and technologies in milk, ice cream, and cultured dairy products. For example, I conducted a six-month evaluation of a new freezing process owned by Rich's in Buffalo, New York. I coordinated research teams and chaired the evaluation committee for that.

A typical week for me involved boarding a plane in the early morning in Houston and flying to Syracuse, where I would be met and whisked to the research offices. There, the men on the research staff (all men!) would be seated around a conference table, waiting for my arrival. I would take my seat at the head of the table, we would have lunch, and the review meeting would begin.

One of the things we were exploring was how cottage cheese could be used if we added a binder to the curds, instead of cream, to make the cheese semi-firm. Once the scientists had accomplished that, we began testing all of the flavors that could be added to it, and found that, just like regular cottage cheese, it blended well with either fruits or vegetables. A lot of testing was done and we were convinced we had a winner with a bar-shaped product that could be eaten out-of-hand.

Despite our confidence, the cottage cheese bars, like most of the products I helped create for Borden, never made it to market. I like to think that rather than disappointments, life offers us learning experiences; even so, I must say that a person had to be a supreme optimist to enjoy that job.

My job with Borden involved even more traveling than I had done with Jenn-Air. I went to New York City a few times each month, and eventually ended up traveling all over the world, locating products and processes for Borden to license. I met with developers and looked at ice cream specialty products in France, Denmark, and Norway. My responsibilities included coordinating the production and test markets for any of Borden's new ice cream products, including three I had created. And again, I had to really know my stuff, because I was the only woman executive among ten thousand Borden Dairy employees. It was quite an adventure!

Another challenge about living in Houston was developing a social life outside of work. My one friend who lived there, Linda Kay, was gracious enough to include me in her family gatherings for holidays, which was especially important during my first year. As time went by and I began to meet a few women in the course of daily life, such as my banker, I organized what I called the "Saturday Group." About eight or ten of us would get together each Saturday to do fun and crazy things that we wouldn't do alone. We alternated planning events, and because we all had such diverse backgrounds, the event was always a surprise, ranging from a cooking lesson, a session in a meditation "tank," to a "play date" in the back room of a fur shop.

This group became my stability lifeline. Because of my hectic schedule and the extensive traveling I did, it took me awhile to realize that I had to have advance plans for my weekends or I would end up home alone. Not good. We women in the Saturday Group loved and supported each other, and taught each other new ideas. It was the very best of a girlfriend relationship.

I was in Houston until 1982, at which time I was transferred to Columbus when Marvin Herb was named president of the combined Food and Dairy Divisions. My first responsibility in Columbus was to manage a major new product. However, soon after I began working in the corporate offices, Marvin left the company when he purchased Coca-Cola Indianapolis, Chicago, and Milwaukee. It was a good fit for him, as his real love had always been the bottling business, so I was pleased for him.

Unfortunately, the vice president I was transferred to was neither a Marvin Herb fan, nor did he like the Marvin Herb "people." Not a good situation for me. He gave me as rough a time as he possibly could, essentially stripping me of many of my projects. I believe he hoped I would quit in frustration if he gave me nothing to do, but he hadn't counted on how tenacious I could be when I set my mind to something. I was more determined to hang in there than he was to discourage me, and I stuck it out. Eventually, he assigned me to work in strategic planning for the combined divisions, but then went so far as to kill the project I was to manage.

In spite of the less-than-ideal conditions at Borden, life wasn't too bad. I bought a beautiful home in a wooded area overlooking a small lake, north of Columbus. I also joined Toastmasters, which gave me an opportunity to meet a wide range of people, both male and female. Because Toastmasters required members to give a speech each month, it helped keep the public-speaking part of my brain well engaged. By then, Mark had graduated from college and was working in Denver. Stewart moved in with me (the house had an apartment on the lower level) in order to attend Ohio State University.

My new job involved strategic planning for the combined food and dairy division. It wasn't as exciting as being director of new product development, but it was still interesting — and still challenging. Because so many people worked at Borden's corporate office (unlike the small number of staff at Houston) I was able to make friends with several people there. My home was very conducive to entertaining, with a pool and hot tub down the hill by the lake that was for the use of the ten or twelve residents of my subdivision. It was a social stretching time; I dated a lot and began to wonder if I would ever remarry.

Being a teacher is simply and absolutely part of what I am, and as I grew professionally, I developed a desire to work with other women toward empowerment. So, during the time I lived and worked in Columbus, I also began, independently, giving workshops for women on how to succeed in business. I used my vacation days to travel to Dallas, Denver, and other major cities for the workshops, and I hired an assistant to manage the details. This concept was an outgrowth of the speeches I had given to women's groups while traveling for Jenn-Air. Because of my connection to home economists through the Jenn-Air distributors, I would ask them to make arrangements with their Home Economists in Business groups.

My keynote speech for these workshops was called "Seven Steps to Success." It was a great professional growth experience for me as I continued to explore and learn everything I could about being successful in business. For many years afterward, I would occasionally meet women in airports and other places who would approach me, saying, "You probably don't remember me, but the speech you gave in Atlanta (or wherever) changed my life." I felt blessed to know that the words God had led me to write and speak had reached willing ears.

All the time, my position with my manager at Borden was becoming increasingly adversarial. He used every trick in the book, from attempting to make my life miserable at work to even infringing on my personal time. I had begun a journal outlining his behavior from the beginning, including dates and descriptions. After a while it became apparent that I was not the only recipient of his harassment; men were kept firmly under his thumb, too. They were reluctant to complain, however, because they couldn't afford to lose their jobs.

In 1984, after two years in Columbus, I decided to leave Borden and move back to Indianapolis to start my own business. It seemed to be the right time to be near my home base. My dad had died and my mother wasn't well; I wanted to live closer to her.

I felt I had to do something about the abusive manager, however. I knew I couldn't afford a lawsuit, so I devised a plan to get my journal to the president of the company.

I put the journal into an envelope and dropped it into the company's internal mail just before the company's five p.m. quitting time. I didn't write "Personal" on the envelope, figuring that way the president's secretary would read it first and share the information with other secretaries.

I had already cleaned out my office the previous weekend and had turned in my resignation. I would be departing at the end of the following day.

Shortly after arriving at work the next morning, I was summoned to human resources. The director inquired about my intent regarding the journal, and I said I wanted only two things. First, that the manager would be forced to cease his abusive behavior, and second, that the damaging things he had put into my personnel file would be expunged. (Another executive friend had tipped me off about the file.)

The end result was that he was chastised by the company president, and I was assured that the bad behavior came to an end. Also, my personnel file was impeccable when I moved on. What I did took courage, but it paid off, and I learned later that my former coworkers began referring to me as the "Joan of Arc" of the company.

The workshops I had conducted in Columbus had been successful and had in a way inspired the concept for my new business, which I called Women's Investment Network (WIN). In my interaction with other women I had observed that both single and married women often knew little, if anything, about finances and financial planning. WIN's mission was to offer services to women to provide knowledge and understanding of money management.

In the meantime, and fortunately for me, when my old boss Louis Jenn learned I was returning to Indianapolis, he contacted me to see if I'd be interested in doing freelance work for him again. He had sold Jenn-Air and started a lot of enterprises. It was a great opportunity for me because it provided income while my business was in the start-up stage. One of the principles I had learned from other entrepreneurs was to pay yourself last — if at all — until your business begins to generate enough income to justify your own salary.

I found an office space for WIN that would accommodate private areas for interviews and counseling, as well as a large room for information meetings and workshops. The concept was that when a woman joined WIN (there was a membership fee), she would be able to meet with our certified planner to assess her finances. We would then help her determine savings and retirement goals based on her situation. We had numerous programs with speakers, and workshops on everything concerning money: insurance, stocks and bonds, how to read financial pages in the newspaper, how to work with your bank, and estate planning, including wills. Women loved it! At last, here was a safe environment where they could ask any question without feeling foolish or being patronized. My own role was to promote the business and recruit new members. In time, we were even able to offer low-cost term insurance and credit cards in a member's own name.

Even in the early 1980s, this was a concept ahead of its time, no doubt about it. Women were just beginning to move into higher-paying jobs and to feel a sense of autonomy and independence. One of the biggest challenges was helping married women whose husbands totally controlled their money. Many of them had no idea if a will existed or what would happen to them if they were widowed or divorced, and we advised them on steps to take to protect themselves and their future security.

CHAPTER 9

Love Changes the Destination

One of the most valuable business tools I had discovered when
I returned to Indianapolis was a publication called *Indianapolis
Business Journal*. I still had a relatively high profile in the community, and I was featured in an advertisement in the *IBJ* endorsing it as
"must" reading for women in business. As a result, when *IBJ* sponsored a pig roast in August of 1985 to thank its advertisers and special friends, I was invited. Little did I know that God had evidently
decided it was time for a change in my personal life.

At that time, WIN was going great and the future looked rosy.
I wasn't all work and no play, though. I had an active and fulfill-
ing social life, and I had dated quite a bit during the almost ten
years I'd been single. I hadn't met anyone I felt I could be serious
about, though, and, at age fifty-one, I had pretty much decided I was
through with dating.

At one point in the afternoon, our hostess drew me aside to introduce me to John Burkhart, owner of the *IBJ*. My heart lurched,
and I knew instantly that this man would be my husband!

I knew of John Burkhart, and we even shared a few things in
common in that my sons and John's two oldest grandsons had gone
to school together and had often played and visited at each other's
homes. Furthermore, John's daughter Gay had been my younger son
Stewart's Cub Scout den mother. All I knew about his marital status
was that he was widowed when his first wife died, and that he had
remarried. At the pig roast, John and I enjoyed chatting about my
family's connection to his family; at least *I* enjoyed it. Probably nothing more would have come of it except the following day I told a

friend about the fabulous older man I'd met. (I was amazed when I learned he was *twenty-six* years older, because he definitely didn't look his age.)

"It must have been John Burkhart," she said.

I was shocked. "What prompted you to think it was John?" I asked.

She didn't answer my question, but did agree that he was indeed fabulous. She then further shocked me by telling me John was recently divorced from his second wife and that he spent a lot of time at my friend's home, because he played tennis with her husband. "Why don't the four of us have dinner together sometime?" she asked. "I'll arrange it with John."

Due to conflicting schedules, it took two months to set up the dinner. John and I hit it off immediately, just as we had at the pig roast. He was charming, witty, and delightful. I was overwhelmed that finding the perfect man had been so easy, but I have always known in my heart that a force beyond our control — God — brings us the most wonderful gifts when we least expect them.

From then on, John pursued me with gusto (although, I must admit, I didn't put up much, if any, resistance). We dined together most evenings and did things together on weekends. Wow! I couldn't believe how lucky I was to have this happening to me! As for John, I don't know if it had been love at first sight for him as it had for me, but he sure acted like it.

My family was supportive of my romance, including my oldest brother, Jim, who had known John for years through Indiana Chamber of Commerce activities. And both of my sons thought he was super. Elder son, Mark, lived in Minneapolis with his bride, Suzy, and when they came to visit me over the Thanksgiving holiday and met John, they immediately gave their stamp of approval. Younger son, Stewart, lived in Indianapolis, so was able to spend a lot of time with us. He, too, was pleased about my turn of events. Without their approval I would not have proceeded with the relationship.

At first, however, not everyone was enthusiastic about my "match made in heaven." Several of my friends thought he was too old for me, but once they met him they succumbed to his charm and their qualms disappeared.

He certainly was the "real thing" as far as I was concerned, and the longer we knew each other, the many qualities of his character proved it to me. He was a man of his word: if he said he was going to do something, he did it. Whenever he came to pick me up for a date, he was right on time. Although he had many accomplishments, he was a humble soul and never bragged or boasted, and he never flaunted his intellect and brilliant mind. He always gave more than he took, and derived great pleasure from helping others achieve their dreams. He was witty and always had a twinkle in his eye, but he never told dirty jokes, nor did he gossip or spread rumors about other people. As I got to know him better, I presumed he was wealthy, but he didn't talk about that, either. In fact we never talked about money, his or mine.

John believed in taking care of himself. He was mindful of his weight and was slim and elegant at six feet, two inches. He helped maintain his trim shape by playing tennis on weekends, a game he learned to play at the young age of sixty-five. He played with a vengeance, preferring the more challenging singles, and kept it up until a knee problem forced him to retire his racket when he was eighty-seven. He could have taken up golf then, but, well, he thought that was a total waste of time.

When it came to his work, John was supremely well organized in everything he did. He also did all of his own typing and secretarial work, using his beloved IBM Selectric typewriter. He was neat and tidy, and his desk work surface was empty at the end of every day.

He had a deep devotion to his country. During World War II he was unable to serve in the military because of his eyes (he wore glasses), so he interrupted his career in Indianapolis and moved with his wife and two young children to Milwaukee where he managed an industrial plant that made a specialized product used by the Navy.

This interruption in his work life was fortuitous. He and some colleagues had worked for Lincoln National before the war broke out, selling life insurance to graduating college seniors. When all of his partners departed to assist in the war effort, they closed their office, but of course the premiums continued to be paid on the policies. After the war, they reconvened and discovered they had enough money in the bank to start an agency of their own, and by 1946 they secured enough financing to start the College Life Insurance Company of America, headquartered in Indianapolis. Eventually they built their own office building at Thirty-fourth Street and Central Avenue. It grew and grew and a second business was added, University Life Insurance Company, which operated in forty-nine states by the time they sold it in 1979.

By the early 1960s they were running out of space in their location. They decided to buy a several-hundred-acre tract of farmland on the far northwest side of town just north of Eighty-sixth Street and bordered by Michigan Road on the west and Ditch Road on the east. It was literally out in the middle of nowhere with no development anywhere near, and the pundits called it "Burkhart's Folly." John ignored the naysayers and proceeded with his plans, hiring an architect from Boston to design their new building.

John loved new ideas as much as he loved the classics. Even so, the architect's drawings showing a radical new concept in office buildings took him by surprise. The design showed nine gleaming pyramid-shaped structures joined together by connecting passages, each with multiple floors. The buildings had windows only on the south side facing a small lake. It was spectacular! Approval was given and construction began on the first three.

The area was christened College Park and the streets were named for Hoosier colleges and universities — DePauw (John's alma mater), Vincennes, and Purdue. John also conceived the idea that it would be a good place for fraternities and sororities to locate their national headquarters. (At least nine are located there now.) Realizing the value of hotel accommodations in the area, John and his partners convinced Holiday Inn to build there. Before long, "Burkhart's Folly" began to become a community unto itself, with homes built on the east side toward Ditch Road, and apartments and condominiums creating a buffer between the homes and the office park. All in all, it was a massive project and John loved every minute of his very busy life. In the end, however, only the first three pyramids were built because when the insurance companies became computerized, John and his partners discovered that they didn't need the additional office space that six more buildings would have provided.

I loved hearing him tell the stories about the birth and growth of College Park. He never lost his attachment to it and continued to maintain an office in the Pyramids until the late 1980s, long after he had sold the insurance companies and other businesses had moved into the buildings.

After we were married, John and I continued to discover that we were alike in so many ways. We were both avid readers, and we both felt a strong commitment to our community and working to enhance its strength and its growth. He admired my courage to try new endeavors, many that I had created. We both liked to finish what was started and we didn't care for loose ends.

He also had come from a rural background. John was born in Tipton, Indiana, north of Indianapolis, where his father was a Disciples of Christ minister. When John was a toddler, his father became ill with tuberculosis, and because there was no cure for the disease then, the doctor suggested they move to a hot, dry climate. Therefore, little John, his mother, and his ill father boarded a train that took them to Colorado City, Texas (near Amarillo). They had little money, so John's mother sold religious books and Wearever Aluminum kitchen utensils door-to-door, while John stayed at home with his sick father. Knowing John, I imagine he did more of taking care of his father, rather than the other way around. Reverend Burkhart eventually recovered enough to be able to preach again, and he served a church there in Colorado City, and later another one in a nearby town.

Reverend Burkhart's health worsened when John was about ten years old, however, and the family returned to Tipton, where they lived with John's paternal grandparents.

When John was twelve years old, his only sibling, a sister, was born. His father died two years later, and John became the head of his family. It was necessary for him to assist his mother in supporting them, so while they lived with his grandparents, he worked after school to make some money for them instead of participating in after-school sports. He was a highly intelligent and hard-working student who had been advanced two grades in his Texas school. Even though he was two years younger than his Indiana classmates, he continued to excel in school, and his high school principal helped him get a scholarship to DePauw University. Room and board were not included in the scholarship, however, so he made an agreement with a fraternity to allow him to live there in exchange for keeping its financial books. He loved DePauw and was a major lifelong supporter of the university.

John and I both loved to travel, and for Christmas when we were dating, he gave me a membership to Ambassadair, a local travel club. He bought a membership for himself, too. A few weeks later he suggested that we take a trip to Spain in late March. I told him I would think about it. I did, then explained to him that I neither wanted nor needed to be known as "John Burkhart's girlfriend," and that the only way I would travel with him was if we were married.

"Then let's get married!" he said.

We had known each other for only six months, but it felt like we'd been together forever.

John was a true romantic, and wasn't content with just material displays of affection. He also indulged me with love poems, such as the one he wrote for our first Valentine's Day together that included a reference to how we met.

It's a time of joy for Hallmark,
And for chocolate candies, too;
For roses red that light the dark
And for fancy bottled brew.

But for some of us it's question time,
Seeking answers we can't find;
Concealing through a crafted rhyme
The puzzles that afflict our mind.

Why was there reserved for me
The lively, loving lass, Lorene?
Why was it meant for me to be
In such a role in such a scene?

On this the Day of Valentine,
I will once more say
How glad I am the memory's mine
Of a certain pig on a certain day.

We decided to have a very small wedding. In Indiana it takes five people — the bride and groom, two witnesses and someone who is qualified to marry you. John's daughter Gay and my son Stewart agreed to be witnesses, and my longtime friend, the Reverend Richard Hamilton, consented to marry us in the chapel of North United Methodist Church at Thirty-eighth and Meridian streets in Indianapolis.

The only glitch was that Reverend Hamilton forgot to come. After waiting by the church doors until five after six for the six p.m. wedding, we made a hasty call to him. He lived nearby so he was there in ten minutes — in suit and tie; he must have dressed in the car. The ceremony was brief. No one was needed to give the bride away and there was only one ring, mine. John didn't like to wear any jewelry except his wristwatch.

Regarding my ring, a couple of weeks prior to the wedding I

had quizzed John about it. He looked blank, then sheepishly admitted that he had given it no thought at all. I then explained that I had taken care of the problem by visiting a local jeweler, and together the jeweler and I had designed a lovely piece that incorporated the diamond from my first engagement ring. That was surrounded by small matching diamonds, which I had traded for some odd-sized ones I had in rings that I never wore.

John loved to tell people that it was the best bargain of our marriage. When we went to the store to pick it up, the young jeweler was shocked to see John Burkhart with me. He told us that he grew up in the neighborhood of John's magnificent home and that he would sometimes pull into the driveway when he was on a date and tell the girl that it was his home. We all had a good chuckle.

We invited a small group of friends and family to join us for dinner at John's country club after the wedding but we hadn't filled them in on anything. We felt we had to be somewhat secretive because it would have been difficult to select only a few guests for such an occasion. The dinner guests were very surprised and happy for us. We left for Spain the next day.

Because the trip was a group venture of the travel club, most of the people were from Indianapolis, several of whom we both knew. One couple we met during that week became very close friends, who later traveled a lot with us. The husband of the couple was even more of a conservative Republican than John, so they got along well.

The honeymoon was the beginning of my shopping extravaganzas, while John trudged along carrying the shopping bags.

John had an impish streak, and on our honeymoon he mailed a card to our tardy minister addressed to "The Late Reverend Hamilton." In the message he said we had planted a "memorial" tree in his honor in Spain.

When we returned from the honeymoon it was time to go home shopping. We both owned condos, but neither was large enough for us together. I didn't want to live too far from the center of our activities, so we were pleased to find a lovely home in a secluded area. The lot had two acres of woods behind it that ended at the White River, and the home was very spacious. It didn't take long for me to realize that even when we combined our furnishings there wasn't enough to fill the space we had. Fortunately, I found a convenient solution for furnishing the large living room. I had visited the Decorators' Show House that year and realized that the living room was almost identical in size to our empty room. I dragged John to see it, he liked it, and we purchased everything, lock, stock, and barrel — including the draperies! We went from empty to completed in one day. The lovely house was our home for four years.

Also, around this time, I decided I wanted, just for a change and just for a while, to try not working at a career. Besides, for the first time in so many years, I didn't *have* to work for a living. As a result, I closed Women's Investment Network. I've had a few regrets about that, and have often wondered how far the business would have gone. In hindsight, I wish rather than closing it I had sold it so it could have continued to operate.

John was a true romantic and wrote several poems for me. This poem was for my first birthday after our marriage.

To My Lorene

Birthdays once were held quite dear
Because they came but once a year.
But each twelve months doth seldom bring
A new wife with her newest ring
So birthday girls take second place
To wives who've won the latest race
But when the wife is still brand-new
And brings to life a birthday too,
You have in hand a combination
That far exceeds imagination.
So here tonight we celebrate

The end result of our first date,
And hope you continue, dutifully
To age so very beautifully.

For my birthday in 1988 I was treated to another verse, this one not so "mushy" but more on the whimsical side.

I am going to write the book on
Loving Older Women since each
July 11th I find I love you more.

On our fifth anniversary, John presented me with another love poem.

A Time for Celebration

Five fabulous years — no more — no less —
Each filled to the top with happiness.
The dreams I had have all come true,
And all because of a wonderful you.
To Decker I owe more than I can repay
And the debt is getting bigger with each passing day.
If you are half as happy as I find myself to be
We'll provide the marriage model for the whole wide
world to see.

We did our best to present our marriage model to the whole wide world. I was no longer tied down to a job, and John did his own thing, so we could come and go as we pleased and indulge ourselves in as much traveling as we wished. We traveled through the Pacific, including Hawaii, Thailand, Singapore, Hong Kong, South Korea, Australia, and New Zealand. We visited Israel, South Africa, South America, and China. On various trips to Europe we toured Italy, Switzerland, Portugal, Spain, France, and Ireland. We enjoyed a number of cruises, including a Mediterranean/Black Sea cruise, a river boat trip on the Elbe River originating outside Potsdam and ending near Prague, which we then visited, along with Budapest. We took an Alaska cruise, a *Queen Elizabeth II* cruise to England with a return on the Concorde, a Panama Canal cruise, and a Hawaiian Island cruise. We didn't neglect the wonders of our own country, though, and traveled extensively within the United States.

Because of our wanderlust, we didn't want to be limited to one vacation location, so we hadn't even considered buying a vacation home. Well, that changed quickly on a visit to friends in Naples, Florida, in 1991. We were so impressed with their breathtaking high-rise condominium building on the Gulf of Mexico that by the time we left we had purchased a condo in the same building. We owned it for six years and enjoyed it tremendously.

Our extensive traveling made the big house in Indianapolis too much to deal with. It required a full-time housekeeper and a groundskeeper that we shared with our next-door neighbor. We looked at several condo possibilities and settled on the sixteen-story Tarkington Tower at the corner of Fortieth and Meridian streets. We decided to purchase three units and put them together to create a spacious penthouse home on the top floor of the building. The city lay spread out below us, providing magnificent views from our windows. The building also had a round-the-clock doorman, as well as a maintenance staff and indoor parking. I thought I had died and gone to heaven!

We entertained extensively and our guests seemed to enjoy our home as much as we did. It was convenient to John's office, which he had moved to a downtown building he jointly owned that was only a fifteen-minute drive away.

We lived in the condo for seven years, but by then, as my grandchildren grew, I realized that their play area was very limited and once again I longed for green space. John agreed to move again, even though he loved the penthouse. His driving was becoming unsafe, so we decided he should close his downtown office and work from home. I found a house on the Northside that was next door to close friends. It featured a big backyard, a small lake stocked

The love of my life, John Burkhart, and me on our wedding day.

The lovebirds honeymooning in Seville, Spain.

Around and around the world we went . . .

John with unmarried (left) and married (right) new friends in South Africa.

In front of the Colosseum in Rome

and Florence's spectacular panorama.

Me with a whaling tripot, New Zealand.

John and a totem of sorts in Bogota, Colombia.

Everywhere we went, I shopped and John schlepped, made a little easier in China with the bicycle-powered shopping cart.

"The Princess" posed as an empress in China with my dashing warrior "king."

Last laugh! John discovered the train from Switzerland to Venice didn't have any shops!

It didn't matter what was under the Christmas tree. John's and my greatest gifts were the smiles and kisses we always had for each other.

When you're in love, you're in love. Our tenth anniversary.

with fish, and it was in a quiet neighborhood with no through traffic. I set about renovating it and we moved in 1996. John's office was in a lovely large room on the lower level that also included a living room, kitchen, bedroom, and bath. I figured that if we ever needed to have live-in help we would be ready for it. It was a terrific location.

The house was also close to the hospital. John's health was unbelievable. He required prostate surgery a year after we married, his first time in the hospital since he'd had pneumonia when he was in college. He continued in good health until he suffered a heart attack in January 1996. The angioplasty procedure was done quickly enough to avert damage to his heart. He was chomping at the bit to return to his office within a week or so after his hospital visit. He did need to be tested every week, however, so the hospital's proximity was a great convenience.

John worked at his office desk every workday that we were in town. Before that, when his office was away from home, he would leave at seven a.m. and return at six p.m. He wrote a weekly column for the *IBJ* for eleven years, then switched his columns to a monthly magazine, *CEO*, when he became the co-owner; he wrote those on the weekends. He had many business interests that required his attention and he kept his own financial records in detail, by hand.

He sold the chain of business journals in 1986, only five years after the business began. Because they had been very successful, he had resources to spread around, which he certainly did by investing in several start-up enterprises, some successful and some not. I never knew any of the details, though, because John was a private person who didn't discuss his finances with anyone, including me. (He did hire a professional accountant to do his taxes.) Until his death he continued his involvement in a variety of enterprises.

Just because I wasn't involved in a career didn't mean I didn't work. I entered a new phase of my life with a plan to focus on volunteer civic involvement. Even so, it wasn't too long before the entrepreneurial bug bit me again.

I had such a good time decorating the home John and I bought, and had received so many compliments, that I decided to launch a home remodeling business. John and I would purchase a house we thought had good turnaround potential, give it a cosmetic fix-up, including landscaping, then sell the house at a price that would net us a profit. (My real estate broker's license that I obtained in the early 1970s and maintained through the years really came in handy for this enterprise.) The first three houses we worked on sold quickly, but the fourth one stood on the market for several months, which wiped out all our profits from the others. Ah, well. So much for Plan A; but there's always something else down the pike.

My last career venture came about totally by accident. In 1991, one of John's former employees in the publishing business had contacted me about buying stock in his fledgling enterprise of five small newspapers. I invested in one called *The Register,* which focused on the activities of social and nonprofit organizations in our area. After only one issue, however, the business fell apart and, as I was its sole investor, I was left as the paper's owner. I probably would have walked away from it and declared it as a loss on my taxes, but John had other ideas. He believed that I should build the paper into an ongoing concern. *The Register* had no office, no assets, and no advertising contracts. So here I went again, building something from scratch and going back to work. But I'd faced challenges like this before and didn't hesitate to take this one on.

First, we looked for office space, and were lucky enough to find some we could rent that included all of the furnishings and equipment from a defunct publishing company. Then I hired the former editor, production coordinator, and a salesperson from that original business, and we kept the contract from the printing company they had dealt with. I also hired a part-time office manager/do-everything person. We were under a crushing deadline but still managed to get the next month's issue out and distributed.

The Register was a free monthly magazine in newspaper tabloid form whose total operating revenue came from advertising. Over the course of the next six years, our staff grew to twelve and circulation grew to more than one hundred thousand; we changed it to a "slick," instead of newsprint, publication, and it became a mainstay in the nonprofit community. Meanwhile, I was the publisher, one of the community events photographers, editorial writer, and chief worrier. John was the financier. I also created a unique delivery system using the *Indianapolis Star* services. *The Register* never really made a profit, but it made a huge contribution to the community. Because of its focus on philanthropy, it was a real boost for fund-raisers. John and I ran the paper for six years, and sold it in 1997. Sadly, the buyer decided not to continue with it.

⁓

Once again, I looked forward to spending more time with my husband and limiting myself to civic work only. But once again, my plans took a back seat to what God had in mind.

John kept his hand in the publishing field, and for several years partnered with a couple of former *IBJ* employees to produce two monthly business magazines, *Indianapolis CEO* and *Columbus* (Ohio) *CEO*. We received a shock in 1997 when John's business partner informed him that the publications were seriously in debt, including owing back taxes. What were we to do?

John and I were faced with real adversity, and we had to make a decision. The easy thing to do would have been to declare bankruptcy and walk away. John had not been in charge of day-to-day operations for the business, and it was not he who had made the mess. Regardless, his name was on the business and neither of us felt that it was the responsible thing to do to leave others holding the financial bag and incurring debt and hardship because their bills were not paid. That just was not in either John's or my makeup, so I found myself rolling up my sleeves and going back to work in order to return the magazines to some form of solvency.

Fortunately, we were able to sell the Ohio publication. We continued publishing the Indianapolis magazine through the following year until we were able to pay off its debts, which were considerable. It was definitely not a happy experience, but we were at least able to face ourselves in the mirror each day with pride, knowing we had done the right thing.

John and I continued to have an active life, and in 1999, at the age of ninety-one, he still worked at his desk daily. Nevertheless, his last year was increasingly difficult as his energy level, mental alertness, and overall physical health began to deteriorate.

One evening we were out to dinner with his daughter and two women from Russia who were our houseguests when John complained of a headache. He quickly became disoriented and we called 911. At the hospital, he lost consciousness during a brain scan. He never regained consciousness, and he died at seven-thirty the next morning.

John's and my marriage was filled with love, laughter, and happiness. Most important, it was filled with trust. Looking back, I see so many similarities between John and my father. They always gave their all in any situation. They were highly intelligent, but didn't take themselves too seriously. And they both had the ability to bring out the best in me and to help me achieve at higher levels than I ever would have dreamed. They loved me completely and unconditionally and they made me feel totally secure and well-grounded. From them, I learned how to be loving and caring while still maintaining my own sense of well-being.

My fourteen years with John proved to me that God's plan is always more wonderful than anything we could ever conceive.

CHAPTER 10

Is That the Garage
Up Ahead?

I suppose you could say that when I went off to college, I was continuing the pioneering spirit that had been so much a part of my family for so many generations.

My dad was the epitome of a pioneer, defined in the dictionary as a person who originates or helps open up a new line of thought or activity in a territory. He seemed not to feel constricting boundaries, but followed his heart and his goals to wherever they might take him.

My mother was truly an accidental pioneer, however, because she was nudged and sometimes pushed into a leadership role not of her choosing. Her pioneering spirit was defined by her willingness and her faithfulness in carrying out her unchosen responsibilities.

These two examples of pioneering were powerful motivators for me, and gave me the strength and courage to forge ahead even when the challenges that were presented to me seemed daunting.

Now that I'm in my early seventies, I suppose I could sit back and relax, be one of those "ladies who lunch." I like lunching, but I also like to keep dreaming. Even though I no longer have to work for a living, I find that I need to work in order to live well. That surely has a lot to do with what my brothers and I refer to as the "McCormick work ethic," which was bred into us from early childhood. The difference is that my work now is focused on giving back.

My parents instilled in my brothers and me from day one the importance of giving to our community and aiding those less fortunate than us. After my marriage to John in 1985, I had all of the philanthropy ingredients at my disposal: time, talent, and resources. John shared my philosophy of giving, and he willingly supported my endeavors and enabled me to give to my community in every way.

I've always loved learning, and I have shared that love by helping make it possible for others to learn. One of my biggest thrills was to provide the original funding of $1 million to establish the Center for Families at Purdue University. The mission for the Center states, "Families form the cornerstones of our society, affecting our growth and development as persons and as a nation. Families provide the basis for self-esteem, communication, and the lifelong desire to learn and work in an increasingly complex society. As children, we need the care of a family to survive. As adults, we depend on family for strength, support, and personal growth."

In April 2004, at the tenth-anniversary celebration of the Center's establishment, we acknowledged another $2.5 million in gifts and seventy grants, making the institution one of the most successful of its kind in the nation. It has grown to become a resource on family information for the Indiana state legislature as well as on other related national issues. Being a part of something that reflects my own belief in supporting families has brought me great pleasure and satisfaction.

Also at Purdue I was honored to serve as Chairman of The President's Council to be a member of the university's first fundraising campaign, which generated more than $300 million for the school, and again, on the following campaign that raised more than $1 billion.

My volunteer support for colleges hasn't been limited to my alma mater. I have also served on the Vincennes University Foundation Board, as a trustee of the University of Indianapolis, and on several advisory boards for Indiana University.

My organizational and conceptual skills in fund-raising and problem-solving have been used for various nonprofit organizations in the community. One of those was Meals on Wheels. In the early

1990s, when I was president of the Indianapolis chapter, it became increasingly difficult to find volunteers to deliver meals to the home-bound. I proposed enlisting the help of corporations or businesses to release some of their employees for noon-time deliveries. The plan proved successful, and now provides most of the volunteer drivers.

I have chaired Methodist Hospital's Individual Gift Campaign for the Foundation, and in 1987, as a member of the hospital's Task Core, I was the founding chair of its annual fund-raiser, the Indianapolis Art and Antiques Show. That event has continued for nearly twenty years and has raised a lot of money for community health projects. I was also the creator and first chair of Grand Bazaar, which has been an ongoing fund-raiser for HealthNet, an organization that serves the health needs of the underprivileged.

It's ironic that I also became involved in the arts considering that I had never attended a symphony, professional theatre performance, ballet, or opera, nor visited an art museum until I was in my thirties. None of these were available in southern Indiana when I was a child, and in my early married years I had neither the time nor the money for such activities. Once I did have the opportunity to participate, however, I really got into it, serving on boards of the Heartland Film Festival, the American Cabaret Theater, the Indiana Historical Society, the Eiteljorg Museum of American Indians and Western Art, and the Indiana Repertory Theatre.

I've always had a passion for fund-raising; I like to organize and to have a beginning and an end to a project, which suits me better than serving as president of an organization. As a result, I have either been the founder, chair, or co-chair for other events including the Indianapolis Symphony Orchestra's Louis Feraud Fashion Show; the Indianapolis Museum of Art's Wine Auction; and the Indianapolis Opera's Home Tour. What I believe is probably my biggest contribution of all was on the Arts Council of Indianapolis, where, from 1988 to 1993, I served as a board member, vice president, and president.

Some projects come about totally by accident. One day I was cleaning out my closet and was wondering what to do with the clothes and accessories I no longer wanted. The obvious answer was to donate them to a worthy cause — but which one? It occurred to me that many of my friends were probably faced with the same dilemma. I contacted Coburn Place, a shelter for abused women and children on Indianapolis' Northside and suggested a clothing sale as a fund-raiser for their cause. They loved the idea. I then contacted more than fifty of my friends and invited them to join the cause. Now, every October, a sale called The Designer's Closet is held in the basement of North United Methodist Church, which is just a few blocks from Coburn Place. It nets more than fifty thousand dollars annually. (Nine years later, I admit that I am not only a donor, I'm also one of the loyal shoppers!)

In 1998, Janet Allen, artistic director at the Indianapolis Repertory Theatre, presented me with a plaque in recognition for my years of service and dedication to IRT.

I had my name in lights — almost — when the Fundraising Executive Organization acknowledged me as volunteer philanthropist of the year in 1990.

The most deeply touching and significant reward, however, was when Purdue University bestowed me with an honorary doctorate in 1997. With me are University president Steven Beering (left) and Dean Dennis Saviano.

CHAPTER 11

Revving the Motor and Running Out of Gas

Throughout my life I have always felt a sense of connectedness, a feeling that has been vital to the development of my values and my self-assurance. Some may call this grounding, others may call it roots, but whatever you might name it, I can't imagine my life without it.

I've often wondered what this means and when it begins. No doubt the security of my farm upbringing played a large role. After all, my brothers and I had the continuity of staying in the same house on the same road in the same community all of our lives while growing up. We attended the same little country church that our extended family in the area did, and the whole family attended the same schools. My brothers and I participated in 4-H — there was never even a discussion about that — and because we all had the same teachers in school, I was known either as Jim and Don's sister or Clarence and Emma's daughter. And, in spite of the fact that my father was gone so much of the time when I was growing up, it was all I ever knew so I never felt disconnected from him.

Change was definitely not a factor in my early life, which makes me wonder why I have gone through so many changes in my adult life. So many people fear change and the unknown, but I never have. Perhaps my sense of stability and connectedness has given me the confidence I needed to explore new territory. At any rate, times sure are different from those of my early years! Now, I not only love change, but embrace every opportunity for change. Embracing it doesn't necessarily mean that I will go forward with a change, but it does mean I can at least consider the possibility and the adventures it may hold.

Feeling connected, for me, also comes from being surrounded by the love and support of not only parents, but grandparents, aunts, uncles, cousins, friends, and teachers, too. All of these connections formed strong bonds that made me a strong person.

As I look back, I often think about my first girlfriends, who also happened to be my cousins. Alice Ann, related on my mother's side, was only a year older than I and lived on a nearby farm, so she became my first and most regular girl playmate. Mary and Betty Marie, from my father's side, were also close to my age, and we stuck close together and played at every McCormick family gathering. I'm still close to them, and they are still among my best friends.

Going through grade school, high school, and college, my connections increased as I met more girls and young women, many of whom I'm still in touch with. That trend has continued through my professional organizations, careers, and nonprofit activities where I have connected with literally thousands of women who I am glad to say have also become good friends.

I suppose you could say connecting is like networking, but I believe that it goes far deeper, much like a tree. Starting from a mere seed or acorn, a sapling casts its roots, connecting to the soil and becoming strong. Birds and animals build their homes in its branches, and people relax in the comforting shade it gives. If those roots are well-nourished and the tree is tended and appreciated, it grows and grows and expands beyond anything that could ever be imagined from looking at that tiny acorn or seed. I like to think that my lifelong connectedness has enabled me to grow strong and help others.

Although the girls and women I've known have been such an important part of my growth, I never would have succeeded without the boys and men. They completed the process of connectedness.

As I have emphasized in this book so many times, my dad had

True connections never die. My cousin and first girlfriend Alice Ann and I are as close as ever.

a huge influence on me. But so did my brothers and all of my male friends. Without them, I doubt I would have felt comfortable with the "only female in the group" role that I played in so many of my jobs. Add to this group my two sons, my two grandsons, and my husbands.

The men who hired me at Ruben, Montgomery Associates, Jenn-Air Corporation, and the Dairy Division at Borden all became friends and mentors. Bob Montgomery helped me develop my creativity and self-confidence. Lou Jenn taught me how to communicate effectively with a minimum of words; and Marvin Herb showed me how to go into the unknown — the great big world out there beyond the Midwest.

Many other men influenced my life — coworkers and colleagues, nonprofit leaders and participants, and teachers and clergymen. I suppose I could mention all the men I have dated during my single days between marriages, too, but I think I'll forego naming names.

Being and feeling connected is a lifelong process. In addition to people and places, I also feel a connectedness through my education. I left Purdue University with a learning foundation that has led me to a series of opportunities and careers ranging from teaching to broadcasting to writing and, ultimately, to being a corporate executive and working in the nonprofit sector. I know that my being a teacher is my core and provides the continuity through every single job I've had.

Foremost and everlasting, however, is my feeling of connectedness with God. Without that, I doubt I would have proceeded very far at all.

Sometimes it becomes necessary to disconnect, to make a change, whether or not it is intentional or even desired. William Bridges, in his book *Transitions: Making Sense of Life's Changes,* states that "changes are driven to reach a certain goal, but transitions start with letting go of what no longer fits or is adequate to the life stage you are in." He adds that the transition begins with letting go of something you have believed or assumed, some way you've always seen yourself, some outlandish perspective on the world, or an attitude toward others. His message is that transition is internal, while change is external, and both require endings that are the first, not the last, act of the play.

If the definition of the word "connect" is to unite or associate with others in relationships, then obviously "disconnect" means to break that tie. This break can occur through anger, deceit, or death, which disconnected me from my parents and my husband John.

My dad suffered from Parkinson's disease for nearly thirty years before his death. Despite two surgeries and the best medical care available, his life was filled with everyday difficulties. This never broke his spirit, though; in fact, the seemingly insurmountable obstacles he faced each day seemed to make him more resolved to make the best of his situation. During those years of his illness he continued to be a vital force in his community, serving in several leadership capacities, including that of president of the board of trustees of Vincennes University. His life was a testament to living with faith and fortitude.

Mother lived four more years after Dad's death, but we actually lost her long before that, as she descended into the depths of Alzheimer's disease. Only a shell remained of that strong woman who raised four children and ran a farm single-handed before that horrible illness claimed her life in 1987.

As sorrowful as it was to lose my parents, John Burkhart's death was my most difficult and painful disconnect. Our marriage and love for each other had been so complete that I couldn't imagine my life without him. I must admit that I often felt his spirit near me, guiding me with business assistance and loving support for months after his death.

I know I can never replace John or my parents or any other person, but I learned to live with my grief, and it became a meaningful transition for the next step in my life. John and my parents are disconnected from me physically, but we will always be connected spiritually because of the love and respect we had for each other. Real love is a bond that never can be truly severed.

As painful as it is to lose a loved one to death, it's not nearly as hurtful as those disconnections caused by the death of a relationship. I learned that bitter lesson through divorce.

Divorce is never a happy event, even if the one who initiates the proceedings does so as the only way to reach the light at the end of a very dark tunnel and the only path to future happiness.

My divorce from George was particularly sad because we had two sons involved. It didn't matter that they were teenagers; the boys were devastated, and I don't believe they have ever recovered from the impact, even thirty years later. Life is never easy, and there's always a sense of regret for what might have been. Fortunately, George and I have always remained on friendly terms, and we both happily remarried.

A few years after John's death, I remarried, and it too ended in divorce. That divorce was extremely difficult for me. As soon as our "I do's" were said, I began to get the feeling that he "didn't." I sensed a lack of commitment from the start and it never got better during the three and a half years we were together. Eventually, the marriage came to an end when he announced that he was divorcing me. I experienced anger, betrayal, disappointment, and grief — grief for the loss of a dream that I had thought would last for the remainder of our lives. It took more than a year of intense suffering, but I finally pulled myself together, straightened up and lifted my head high, and embarked on a new, single life.

Losing a job is another particularly painful disconnection. I remember vividly the only time I was "released from my responsibilities." That experience gave me an "out of body" feeling that left me wondering where to go and what to do. I believe things like this almost always happen for the best, however, so I quickly hooked back up with myself and set out on the next challenge.

Feelings of disconnectedness can be overwhelming, but I've discovered for myself that they actually are only as powerful as I allow them to be. I learned to deal with them the same way I've dealt with other forms of adversity: look it in the face, try to understand where it's coming from, seek outside help if necessary, and, eventually, move on. Without a doubt, the most valuable help I receive is through prayer.

We all contend with losses in life that force us to dig into our faith in God and ourselves to come up with new resolve. As we're faced with adversity we also contend with negativity and negative words such as the "D" words: disappointment, dismay, disillusionment, and disconnectedness. I've learned that by coping with those "D's" I can in time move on to the greatest positive "D" word, "do," as in "*do* something!" and start my way toward recovery.

Peace at the Finish Line

So here I am, into the seventh decade of what I believe has been a wonderful and amazing life. I've met so many people, been so many places, and been involved in so many enterprises, much more than I could ever have anticipated when I was growing up on that farm in southern Indiana.

I guess because of the way things have progressed you could call me an "accidental pioneer." After all, I didn't set out to do many of the things I've done. They seemed to just happen. But I also have to consider how "accidental" my pioneering was.

For me, part of what happened was being in the right place at the right time. An even greater part of it, however, I'm sure, was having a good foundation that prepared me for and a willingness to try new things, a desire to continue to learn, and a commitment to working hard, giving 125 percent. Most important, I kept my faith and trust in God, and have been willing to follow His plan for me.

I'm not unusual in my family. My three brothers also have been creative and adventurous, and all have been successful in all their endeavors. It surely was in our nature, but I can't overlook the fact that our parents were good role models.

I may have crossed many finish lines, but I'm certainly not finished. I can't imagine just sitting back and relaxing, at least not for long. At John's funeral, he was praised for his lifetime of loving service to his family, his community, and his country. I fill the void left in my life from losing him by carrying on his legacy. I've always heard his voice in my ear, and felt God's steady hand guiding me along. Somehow I've always found the time and the energy for one more project or one more meeting to counsel organizations or individuals who asked for my assistance.

If God deems it necessary for me to head up another community project, or even to participate in or own or operate another business enterprise, it would be difficult to say no! After all, the drive through life doesn't end in any particular driveway, but continues as long as you're willing to keep your engines running.

Recipe index